DATE DUE

Toward a Genealogy of Individualism

A VOLUME IN THE SERIES

Critical Perspectives on Modern Culture

edited by David Gross and William M. Johnston

Toward a Genealogy of Individualism

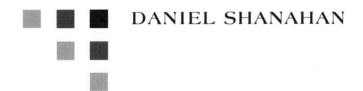

DANIEL SHANAHAN

The University of Massachusetts Press

Amherst

Copyright © 1992 by
The University of Massachusetts Press
All rights reserved
Printed in the United States of America
LC 92-10933
ISBN 0-87023-811-6
Designed by Jack Harrison
Set in Americana and Sabon by Keystone Typesetting, Inc.
Printed and bound by Thomson-Shore, Inc.
Library of Congress Cataloging-in-Publication Data
Shanahan, Daniel.
  Toward a genealogy of individualism / Daniel Shanahan.
    p.   cm. — (Critical perspectives on modern culture)
  Includes bibliographical references and index.
  ISBN 0–87023–811–6 : (alk. paper)
    1. Individualism   2. Self (Philosophy)   I. Title.   II. Series.
HM136.S46   1992
302.5'4—dc20   92–10933
                                    CIP

British Library Cataloguing in Publication data are available.

for Bill Craig
individualist, communitarian, and educator

Contents

Acknowledgments

Lists of acknowledgments are like speeches given at certain awards events: one is never satisfied that one has thanked everyone who contributed to one's success, but the need to get on with things at hand demands brevity.

Insofar as what follows is a success, thanks must be expressed to many people: to Lucio Ruotolo, Thomas Moser, and Ian Watt of Stanford University and Victor Comerchero of CSU Sacramento, for having helped me when I first tackled the topic of individualism a decade and a half ago; to Nenad Miscevic of the Filosofski Facultet in Zadar, Yugoslavia, whose interest in my work helped motivate me to continue it, and who helped arrange the publication of "Toward a Redefinition of Individualism" in *Filosofska Istravinja;* to Karl Pribram of Stanford and Radford universities, Wallace Lambert of McGill University, and Philip Rieff of the University of Pennsylvania, who encouraged me to continue my work on Freud and individualism when the going got particularly rough; and to those who read parts of this and related works and gave me helpful commentary and criticism along the way: Francis L. K. Hsu of Northwestern University, Paula Moddel and Glen Fisher of the Monterey Institute of International Studies, Richard Yarborough of UCLA, Eric Solomon of San Francisco State, and Richard DeBacher of Southern Illinois University Press. Thanks must also go to Mabel Lernoud and Claire DeJunnemann, two secretaries on different sides of the Atlantic but on the same side of the reliability fence. And very special thanks go to Clark Dougan at the University of Massachusetts Press for his support and his encouragement, and to

James Tollefson of the University of Washington for careful and compelling readings of the manuscript.

Finally, no list of acknowledgments would be complete without mention of the former *Statni Bezpecnost,* or Czech secret police—now, happily, more a thing of the past than individualism itself. Their job was to keep foreigners and Czechs sufficiently off-balance to prevent them from interacting with any degree of normalcy or ease. Had they not done that job so well during the year I spent as a Fulbright professor at Charles University, I might have spent all my free time in cafes and pubs, talking endlessly about the subject discussed here rather than writing about it.

Toward a Genealogy of Individualism

Introduction

As Suzanne Langer has said, how one formulates one's inquiries reveals one's attitude of mind. This book is no exception. However, it is perhaps somewhat exceptional in that its mode of inquiry and the attitude of mind it implies are not what some (perhaps many) who pick it up will expect from its topic or its title. For the treatment contained here falls outside the framework of one of the primary modes of the contemporary discussion of individualism, and the differing attitude of mind implied therein bears some explaining.

Contemporary discussion about individualism has taken place primarily in two modes. One is that of Steven Lukes in *Individualism,* David Riesman in *Individualism Reconsidered,* and Louis Dumont in *Essays in Individualism.* Each of these takes a somewhat literalist approach: individualism is treated as a given in the Western tradition, a set of social and philosophical attitudes that can be analyzed and discussed in more or less traditional terms, within the framework of what Thomas Kuhn might call "normal" inquiry.[1] This mode includes both defense (Reisman), critique (Dumont), and objective analysis (Lukes), and it has its strong points, chief among them the ability to uncover and explore some of the features of individualism that inform our social and personal lives, especially the subtly accepted but often unarticulated beliefs that accompany the individualistic frame of mind.

However, it can be rightly said that this "normal"—what we will call traditional—mode of inquiry runs the risk of psychological naïveté: Lukes and Dumont, for instance, ignore Freud completely; the notion that individualism might have some relation to the unconscious or to "absolute, primary narcissism" goes unexplored. Thus, it is not surprising to find a second mode of discussion about individualism, one radically opposed to traditional inquiry, vigorously assertive about the fundamental superficiality and naïveté of traditional analyses of the individual, insistent that the mode of analysis must be transformed, and currently very much in vogue. This "transformational" mode provides both a counterpoint and a contrast to the approach taken in this book. The traditional mode is discussed in chapter 1 below. However, a brief preliminary discussion of the contrasts that exist between the transformational mode and the approach taken in this book may make it easier for those on either side of the various fences involved to digest what is to come.

So radically different is the transformational approach to the individual that any attempt to discuss it is what Herman Melville might have called a "honeyed-head" into which one can easily slip, never to be heard from again. Moreover, any discussion is made more complicated by the fact that, while there may be agreement on the inadequacy and superficiality of the more traditional approach to analyzing the individual, the transforming alternatives differ importantly from one another in ways that, for our purposes, are probably best characterized as falling into two camps.[2] Perhaps appropriately, neither of these two camps has names that identify them in a neatly traditional fashion, and each may overlap with the other at times; but they are probably most frequently differentiated by their members' leaning toward either Marxism (Jameson, Althusser, Habermas, the Frankfurt School) or poststructuralism/postmodernism (Lacan, Foucault, Derrida). We will discuss their differing features in a moment. However, it is first necessary to state the common element that exists between them, for that element represents the most significant departure they make from traditional discussions of the individual.

Regardless of the consequences they draw from their critique of the traditional approach to analysis of the individual and individualism, the more radical contemporary theorists generally start from the premise that the concept of the individual, as the term has been used by traditional analyses, is a *fiction* based on unexamined ideological assumptions about the freedom of the individual that ignore underlying factors so profoundly influential as to render the concept of the individual useless for thoughtful analysis. Put simply, this premise rejects the notion that there is a pristine, universal "self" that exists in existential detachment from everything around it, free to make choices based on unique and individually privileged perceptions to the end of achieving some uniquely individual expression. On the contrary, it is argued, subterranean influences of all kinds, from power relationships to the unconscious, from capitalism to the elusive nature of language and narrative, are so predominant in and intertwined with the life of the conscious entity we call the "self" that any discussion that treats the self at face value is an exercise in the illusory. The discrete individual, taken both in the personal sense and in the historical sense (the entity "liberated" by the march of progress over time) is a fabrication—a *reification*—that dissolves before our very eyes when subjected to the cold scrutiny of methodical analysis. In its own way, each camp sees its mission as the transformation of the contemporary discussion about the individual through the dissolution of the concept of the individual itself—often referred to as the individual subject.[3]

One emphasis encountered in attempts to dissolve the individual "subject" is shared by many in both the Marxist and the postmodernist camps alike: the importance of "power relationships," probably most associated with the work of Michel Foucault. Foucault tries to demonstrate that most of the supposed achievements of individualism recognized by an analyst like Lukes or Riesman—the increase in personal freedom, for instance, or merely a heightened sense of individual traits—are really the reverse of what they appear to be: personal freedom is really only half of a figure-ground dyad that is formed by the constant struggle between power and recalcitrant wills; heightened individualization is simply greater visibility produced by improved surveillance techniques and is therefore far from a contribution to individual dignity and worth. In other words, while history may seem on the surface to have been the story of individual liberation, it is in fact better characterized as a story of personal confinement that emerged as society developed more and better means of asserting its power over the individual.

The attraction of this approach for the Marxist thinker is obvious: one need only add that the society that imposes itself is class based and that the appropriate response is the unmasking of the class-based social oppression that lies at the heart of all power relationships, and one has a classic Marxist interpretation. However, Foucault and most others in the postmodernist/poststructuralist camp part company here. Foucault never makes clear, for instance, where the source of these power relationships lies—whether in individuals, in society, or in the coming together of the first into the second; nor does he necessarily think power relationships are a bad thing; nor does he believe that their unmasking will necessarily lead to the liberation of the human spirit. In fact, there is a deep epistemological gulf separating the two camps at this point. For where the Marxist critique of the bourgeois individual subject is based on the firm belief in a knowable reality based on definable principles (the reality of class struggle, the material base for that struggle, the principle of the dialectical movement of the struggle, etc.), the postmodern/poststructuralist critique of the "subjective consciousness" is based on a much more radical epistemological shift—in fact the dissolution of epistemology itself.

For in response to the question of how we know what we know, the poststructuralist/postmodernist critique posits a permanent uncertainty about whether we really know anything. The intricacies of this argument are too involved to be discussed here;[4] however, the key to the poststructuralist/postmodernist view lies in the role of language in human consciousness and the fact that, since it can be said that we "see" only through the use of language, and since language is itself both a fabrication and a "false copy" of the world around us, its use leaves us in permanent uncertainty about what we really see, what we really know. Moreover, since all our notions about the individual subject are embedded in grand narrative schemes that are simply more elaborately uncertain fabrications, nothing of what we say about the individual can be taken at face value.[5]

This refusal to accept any narrative at face value probably represents the greatest point of irreconcilability between the approach taken by this book and that taken by the poststructuralist/postmodernist wing of what we have here called the transformational school. Not only does the approach taken here not call into question the value of narrative, it is, itself, in large part undertaken in narrative form. The reasons for this contrast can only be sketched here, but they too have language at their root.

In response to the poststructuralist/postmodernist insistence that language is not representative of anything but itself, Walter Ong has said, "It hardly follows that because *A* is not *B*, it is nothing."[6] Language and its more complex form, narrative, are indeed intermediaries between, rather than literal representations of, the world we "perceive." But, as Ong points out, "the structuralists . . . actually—and *unavoidably*—use language representationally."[7] For, whatever limitations language and narrative may bring with them, they remain the only vehicle through which any discussion can take place: if they are fundamentally unreliable, so must *any* argument made through them be.[8] With the poststructuralist/postmodernist critique, one ultimately stands trapped between facing mirrors in which one's image recedes into infinity in either direction, and interpretation becomes a sterile exercise that, as Ong says "can be endlessly titillating, even at those times when it is not especially informative,"[9] but which is not necessarily productive.

The approach taken in this discussion does not presume that language is either representative or unmediating. It does assume, however, that language and narrative can be both self-correcting and self-transforming and that these features, which coexist alongside the limitations with which any writer is familiar, give them the power they carry whether they are used by critic or chronicler.[10] The development of science from Ptolemy to Copernicus to Einstein is a perfect example of the ways in which language, while it may appear to trap us in the limits of its expression at any given moment, actually provides us a means for critiquing the limits of human perception. Written language, especially, provides us with a medium that not only allows critique but encourages it.[11] Put simply, language and narrative, especially in literate form, become, not traps, but the means by which we learn. Thus this discussion is, at least by the standards of some, steeped in narrative. It is not, however, the triumphalist narrative critiqued by members of the transformational school but a narrative of "rise and fall" constructed with the belief that it too can serve as a means to both personal and historical self-awareness.

The questions of personal and historical significance bring us to the Marxist wing of the transformational school, which offers a simpler critique of the concept of the individual subject, one that relies on somewhat more worldly concerns and less on the cognitive doubts evoked by those who find language a hopeless epistemological trap. For Marxists such as Frederick Jameson, language is indeed a trap, but not an inescapable one. For a floor exists beneath the misleading narratives of traditional approaches to the human subject: the reality of oppression. The Marxist critique argues that the grand humanistic narrative of the rise of the individual contained in works like Jacob Burckhardt's *Civilization of the Renaissance* is a fiction, not so much because the true nature of that rise is, à la Foucault, the reverse of what it appears to be, but because the narrative is built on and around bourgeois assumptions that cannot withstand the challenge of a direct confrontation with reality.

Harkening back to Marx's dictum that bourgeois ideology never examines its own premises, this critique argues that the grand humanistic narrative of the rise of the individual is built on a variety of indefensible premises, not least among them the assumption that the intellectual and social evolution of a relatively (and increasingly) small portion of the human population—the Western tradition—represents the totality of human intellectual development through history. At the very least, this argument says, the inadequacy of the sample drawn by such a narrow focus calls into question the validity of its narrative, especially since so much of the Western tradition is based on exploitation of the majority by a privileged few, first within the confines of its own domain ("the West"), and eventually on a global scale. Upon reassessment, one sees that the privileged position given to products of the Western tradition is a "tip of the iceberg" phenomenon: the Western humanistic heritage is revealed as a tiny feature of a much larger narrative scheme that has been unfairly, in Hegelian style, turned on its head. A new, transformational critique requires using the reality of human oppression—and the need to eliminate it—as the foundation for a new assessment of all narrative schemes, and in this critique the concept of the individual subject is given minimal importance because it springs from bourgeois assumptions that simply do not hold true for the majority through human history.[12]

This critique is a formidable one, not because it is couched in Marxist ideological terms, but because it raises an important and difficult question: can the intellectual and social history of a relatively small group be taken to represent the primary achievements of human history as a whole, especially when those achievements are built on a system of inequality and oppression?[13] The simple answer is no. However, to return to Ong's characterization of the poststructuralist/postmodernist critique of language, if *A* is not *B,* it is not necessarily the case that *A* is nothing.

To begin with, it seems highly reductive to make representative size a prerequisite for validity. The fact that the Western heritage springs from a relatively select group of privileged elites, both within the Western context itself and in terms of global history, does not thereby exclude it from having either influence or truth value. Indeed, there are countless examples throughout history of small groups, like the ancient Hebrews or the forest-dwelling ascetics who produced the *Upanishads,* who have an impact on history completely out of proportion to their size. It is also a commonplace that most philosophers, artists, and other "truth-tellers" in human society emerge from privileged social, economic, political, or religious positions because their privilege allows them the opportunity for reflection and expression that the less privileged lack.[14] Marx himself, especially if taken in the global context that had begun to emerge in his time, qualifies as one of those. To disparage the Western concept of the individual subject as a largely bourgeois fiction is as questionable as presenting the grand humanistic narrative of the rise of the individual in the West as the ne plus ultra of the human experience. Something that captures both the importance and the limits of the Western individualistic perspective is called for, and since the discussion contained herein represents an attempt to combine those two, the premises upon which it is built are worth articulating.

We do not seem to balk at the notion that certain societies, especially ancient ones, were able to develop technologies that not only advanced them beyond their contemporaries but allowed them a vast influence that sometimes took the form of domination; in most cases—the development of iron-working techniques in ancient Anatolia, for instance—the use of these technologies for domination does not lead us to question their validity as tools for the enhancement of human existence. We seem less comfortable, however, with treating ideological and philosophical developments in the same way, even though it can be said that both ideologies and philosophies are *technologies*—means to producing ends—which have their validity (the degree to which they reflect an accurate understanding of the nature of things), their influence (the extent to which they are adopted by others), and their limits (the extent to which they must be supplemented with—or even replaced by—other, more comprehensive strategies).

This book is based on just such a perspective: that individualism was a technology developed in response to a universal need that emerged as early civilizations proved themselves too inflexible to maintain coherence as size increased.[15] In place of the rigid, hierarchical, and elite social structures that had proven to be highly useful technologies as the species moved out of its nomadic, tribal phase, a self-motivating, self-directing strategy was gradually adopted that put a powerful tool at humans' disposal: personal initiative. Over the period of two or three millennia, that tool allowed the species to exploit, not only its own talents, but the natural resources available to it—and to such a degree that humanity may now have the ability to provide for and maintain itself in an equilibrium with its environment in the fashion it once did in a more episodic, incidental, and intuitive fashion during its nomadic phase millennia ago.

As is the case with all new technological innovations, however, the adoption and development of this technology had its costs. Chief among them was the fact that it flourished, no doubt partly through chance and partly through the fortuitous combination of circumstances that presented themselves there, in the area we now call Europe, but not in other regions of the world. Consequently, the advantages it brought with it—such as the rapid exploitation of environmental resources that individualism's primary transmission device, entrepreneurial capitalism, made possible—were muted in those areas in which individualism did not flourish, and these same areas eventually fell under the domination of the civilization that had—for the time—the more efficient technology.

Moreover, individualism, like any technology, had its limits—not the least being that, by playing so heavily on one feature of human experience—personal subjectivity—it ignored others that would have given it a more balanced view of the human experience. We are confronting those limits today (see chapters 7 and 8 below), often in crisis fashion, and it may very well be that we will one day—perhaps even soon—come to view the "innovation" of individualism with the same bemusement we now feel when we encounter the ancient Egyptian concept of the god-king. However, to dismiss either the concept of individualism or that of deistic sovereigns as "fictions," bourgeois or otherwise, is to ignore another essential feature of the human experience: humankind lives by its myths.

That we would now treat with great circumspection any claim to either kingly authority or immortality does not change the fact that such concepts represented a powerfully viable force in the civilizations that took them literally, and that those concepts contributed in some fashion to the further development of the species as a whole: the belief that pharaoh could enter a glorious afterlife made possible the belief that we all could, and the latter contributed greatly to increasing our sense of the dignity of human life. In the case of individualism, the fact that its fruits were not spread evenly throughout the species does not obliterate its worth: it merely indicates the shortcomings that accompany it when, as has been the case, it is adopted as a self-sufficient world view.

In one sense, we may be said to live on a historical pivot far more momentous than the shift away from individualism this book suggests in its final chapters, itself a momentous enough event. For the fact that individualism has contributed greatly to the disequilibrium in opportunity that we see in the modern world is much less significant than the fact that we recognize that limitation. Our ability to recognize the shortcomings of one of the major myths of Western civilization may indicate that we have developed the ability to scrutinize our myths and assess where they enrich and where they deplete the quality of human life. If this is indeed the case, it would be a mistake simply to adopt yet another mythological position to counter the shortcomings of one previously held, and therein lies the strongest objection to the dismissal of the "individual subject" as merely a bourgeois fiction.

For if we attempt to counter individualism's shortcomings by painting it strictly as a self-perpetuating rationalization used to justify the subjugation of the many by the few, we ignore the fact that it did much to enhance the possibilities available to us as a species and that, in true dialectical fashion, it planted the seeds of its own destruction in fostering such things as an increasing degree of respect for human dignity and human rights.[16] In other words, if we portray individualism in a one-sided fashion, we really do nothing more than adopt another myth of limited representational value, perhaps at precisely the moment when the ability to select and modify, rather than adopt, the myths by which we live has finally been afforded to us.

Thus, if we are to make a genuine contribution to the wealth of human knowledge, to our ability to assess myths even as we live by them—if we are, in other words, to develop our facility to see clearly on the basis of what we *know,* rather than what we *believe*—it is less important to "unmask" our myths than it is to develop a balanced view of them.[17] To relegate the subjective individual, or the individualistic heritage from which that concept springs, to the category of "mere" (mere bourgeois fiction or mere epistemological fabrication) is to embrace another myth as a means of critiquing one whose shortcomings were for too long hidden from view by that very same believer's embrace.

Readers may thus find themselves confused, at least at first, by the fact that the narrative account presented here seems at times to express enthusiasm and even excitement about a habit of mind it later critiques as inadequate and moribund. The only explanation that can be offered is that the rise of individualism is indeed an exciting spectacle and the opportunities it has opened to humankind dazzling, thus the examination of individualism's genealogy is an invigorating process.[18] If indeed it has helped provide us with the means by which we come to critique and even abandon it, then it is no inconsistency to examine its decline— if not with enthusiasm, then with determined rigor and a well-earned self-confidence. For the dispassion with which we are able to examine individualism's limits is the measure of how much we have benefited from the opportunities it has afforded us.

1
Toward a Redefinition of Individualism

It should not surprise anyone familiar with the subject that the term "individualism" has been used in a variety of ways, none of them necessarily in accord with the others. Common usage—at least in the United States—has tended to make "individualism" a term with very positive connotations, so positive in fact that one might easily find it among the common person's list of those things that can make us great. Indeed, that great common man, Ralph Waldo Emerson, remarked in 1844 that "the Union must be ideal in actual individualism."[1] Yet, when the *Encyclopaedia of the Social Sciences* begins its discussion of the term by calling it an "attitude of mind which is naturally produced in a certain kind of society," it continues, "That society is most easily described in negative terms."[2]

In fact, the term "individualism" opens up a labyrinth of meaning that goes well beyond mere disagreement about positive and negative connotations. Colin Morris's introduction to his *Discovery of the Individual: 1050–1200* reveals a few of the shadowy passages that beckon when one tries to explore the meaning of individualism. He says:

> The hard core of this individualism lies in the psychological experience with which we began: the sense of a clear distinction between my being and that of other people. The significance of this experience is greatly increased by our belief in the value of human beings themselves. Humanism may not be the same thing as individualism . . . but they are at least first cousins, for a respect for the dignity of man is naturally accompanied by a respect for individual man.[3]

Morris's "sense of a clear distinction" between beings is easy enough to accept; he is, in fact, probably completely correct in identifying that sense as the foundation of individualism. But the sense of distinctness of being can lead to many things, not all of them necessarily humanistic; it may as easily lead to opportunism, and worse, if it is not tempered by a "belief in the value of human beings in themselves"—precisely the point upon which negative assessments of individualism, from de Tocqueville to the *Encyclopaedia of the Social Sciences,* hinge, as we shall see. Nor is there any guarantee that the tempering "value of human beings" will follow upon the perception of distinctness. We may like to think that individualism is a form of humanism, but there is not unanimous agreement on this point.

Morris wisely avoids making any sweeping claims about the nature of the relationships between individualism, our belief in the value of human beings in themselves, or the tendency he later ascribes to Kant and others "to assert the supreme value of the individual."[4] Certainly each of the passageways we glimpse in Morris's description does belong to the network of meaning that makes up "individualism," but he does not attempt to provide a map of this labyrinth. And perhaps it is his reluctance to do so that saves him from falling into the trap of treating this complex maze from a single, limiting perspective.

Though it would be unfair to accuse them of reductionism or even of failure to appreciate the complexity of their topic, some discussions of individualism set out to map the labyrinth of its meaning, both connotative and denotative, but, for all their depth of analysis, often leave one feeling that something essential has been left out. For the most part, these discussions tend to be written from the point of view of the social sciences, which appear to have appropriated the term "individualism" for use in a largely political context—an unfortunate circumstance, since, as Morris suggests, the term has connotations that reverberate throughout the broad range of humanistic study.

Louis Dumont's *Essays on Individualism: Modern Ideology in Anthropological Perspective* is one such book, a collection that provides some valuable historical insights into how individualism has taken its place among the motivating principles of modern Western life. But fully two-thirds of Dumont's discussion approaches individualism, as does the discussion in the *Encyclopaedia of the Social Sciences,* from a political perspective. Dumont's discussion revolves around the essentially political question of whether or not individualism can be compatible with modern notions of social responsibility in a liberal democracy. Dumont's conclusion—that individualism is a culturally specific characteristic of Western civilization that does not necessarily have universal currency—is both valid and valuable. However, his analysis betrays such an overwhelming preoccupation with the social institutions that have sprung from the West's individualistic heritage, one is left with the uneasy feeling that the individual has disappeared from the discussion.

Steven Lukes's *Individualism,* both less ambitious and more comprehensive than Dumont's book, attempts to respond in a limited fashion to Max Weber's remark that "a thorough, historically oriented conceptual analysis [of the term 'individualism'] would at the present time be of the highest value to scholarship." Lukes offers discussions of the linguistic variants of the term "individualism" and attempts to analyze what he calls "the basic ideas of individualism": the dignity of man, autonomy, privacy, and self-development, among them. But his analysis is also largely political. He says in the opening sentence of his chapter "The Relations between These Ideas": "The first four unit-ideas of individualism singled out above—respect for human dignity, autonomy, privacy and self-development—are essential elements in the ideas of equality and liberty; and specifically, . . . the idea of human dignity or respect for persons lies at the heart of the idea of equality, while autonomy, privacy and self-development represent the three faces of liberty or freedom."[5] Certainly one can argue that Lukes's four "unit-ideas" are "essential elements" of equality and liberty. However, one must again wonder how complete a picture can be painted when the subunits of individualism are subsumed under political categories that may not even have existed in the Middle Ages, when, as Morris demonstrates, individualistic tendencies were already emergent. Before making any definitive finding about where the subunits of individualism reside today, it would seem appropriate to look a little more closely at how individualism came to be what it is, and not merely within the confines of the political context Lukes and Dumont adopt.[6]

The reason such studies take a political orientation is not hard to find: both Lukes and Dumont are responding, at least in part, to what Carl Becker might call a changing climate of opinion about individualism. More specifically, both men are responding to modern attempts to discredit individualism. Lukes in particular recounts the growing hostility toward individualism expressed in a variety of quarters, from Edmund Burke to Alexis de Tocqueville and John Stuart Mill, and he tries—with limited success—to demonstrate that the "core values of individualism" can be maintained. However, in their decision to develop their analyses from a purely political perspective, both writers minimize the degree to which they treat what Morris calls "the psychological experience" that "lies at the core of individualism"; neither mentions either Descartes or Freud more than in passing. As a consequence, their discussions have a very limited focus.

An essay by David Riesman illustrates the way in which changing attitudes have made objective analysis of individualism difficult and also suggests why analyses that take the political perspective are incomplete. An unapologetic affirmation of the continuing value of individualism in the tradition of Western liberal democracy, "Individualism Reconsidered" defends individualism against what Riesman sees as the encroachment of "groupism"—the tendency to overstate humankind's social nature so greatly as to neglect or even suppress the individual side of human nature. An avowed sociopolitical statement of belief, Riesman's essay is built around a single, primary premise that forms, for Riesman, the ne plus ultra of the individualistic bias; he says, "I am insisting that no ideology, however noble, can justify the sacrifice of an individual to the needs of the group."[7] Here, in simple and very explicit terms, is where Morris's "psychological experience" of "a clear distinction" between one being and another—combined with his "value of human beings in themselves"—comes to rest in the modern, political analysis qua defense/attack of individualism: the distinction between individuals, combined with the value each should place on the other, leads to an affirmation of an atomistic society based on mutual non-encroachment.

Here again, one need not disagree with Riesman's argument to be able to see how little it deepens our understanding of individualism, its genealogy, or its changing place in the contemporary world. When one takes individualism to be nothing more than a benevolent "hands off" policy dictated by an existential value placed on human life and subscribed to by all, one begs the question of what human beings are valued for, and one also ignores what the coming together of individuals that is not "groupism" may tell us about the nature of the individual.

Even if one engages Riesman's assertion of individual inviolateness on its own terms, one is left dissatisfied. Perhaps no individual *should* be sacrificed to the needs of the group on ideological grounds. But what of those who willingly sacrifice themselves? Are they deluded, schizophrenic, transcendent—or none of these? If any of these, what does their sacrifice tell us about the value we place on "human beings in themselves"? Is it possible that those who sacrifice themselves have transcended individualism? If so, are they statistical quirks in an otherwise uniformly self-interested species, or do they point the way to new heights to which, in the right circumstances, any of us might aspire?

Clearly, these difficult questions force us back to an examination of many of our basic premises about human nature. But just as clearly, any discussion of individualism must be willing to engage these questions, and most political analyses of individualism fail to engage them at all. This is not to say that political philosophy does not have something to tell us about individualism: it is just not likely to give us the clearest picture of the profoundly absorbing questions that necessarily underlie the discussion. The assertion or affirmation that the individual must occupy an inviolate position if we are to preserve our humanistic heritage may ring with intellectual courage (though, as Riesman himself admits, it will smack of individual selfishness and irresponsibility for some). But such an assertion does not take us very deeply into the questions of what, given that we are psychological and moral as well as political beings, individualism means for us today, how it came to play that role, or what kind of role it is likely to play in the future.

Because he is writing in response to the question of whether or not individualism can any longer be considered a virtue, Riesman does at least refine our focus on the changing climate of opinion about individualism. For the doubts embedded in this change and the forcefulness with which Riesman feels they must be answered are further evidence of the problematic nature of individualism today. Clearly one of the basic premises in any discussion of individualism must be that it provokes feelings of deep ambivalence. But that fact hardly gives us anything to stand on, for it does little more than establish the fact that we occupy unstable ground. And it does little to define individualism in a way that will allow us to engage any of the deeper questions about its nature. Where are we to turn?

In the face of the overwhelming attention paid to social institutions, as in Dumont, and political philosophy, as in Lukes, it would seem to make sense to turn to the individual perspective itself, to look through the eyes of the creature that has caused all the fuss and learn something about the nature, changing or otherwise, of individualism as seen from that perspective. Unfortunately, there is little contemporary comment from this angle. Morris introduces this perspective with his remark about the "psychological experience" of clear distinctions that exist between beings, but he carries it no further. Dumont discusses the contrast between the "outer- and inner-worldly" focus precipitated by Christianity but quickly subsumes this distinction under the dialectic between private self and social responsibility, with heavy emphasis placed on "political categories."[8] Lukes discusses such things as "ethical" and "epistemological" individualism but sees them as important only insofar as they conflict with or reinforce such social concepts as equality and liberty.[9]

One analysis of individualism does, however, offer us some insight into what individualism means for the individual himself or herself. Ian Watt's *Rise of the Novel* nearly always finds mention in discussions of individualism, largely because of his chapter "Robinson Crusoe, Individualism, and the Novel." However, rarely is the introduction to Watt's book, "Realism and the Novel Form," cited, which is very unfortunate indeed. For not only does Watt here lay down epistemological foundations that allow him thoroughly, yet dispassionately, to cover much of the same ground dealt with in social scientists' discussions of individualism, but the epistemology he introduces greatly enlarges our understanding of individualism. In fact, one might fairly say that Watt uncovers a key element in understanding individualism from the individual's perspective.

In the opening chapter of his book, Watt examines the relationship between realism and the novel—"the form of literature which most fully reflects [the] individualist reorientation." He remarks that the novel's "primary criterion was truth to individual experience," a criterion based on the "general temper of philosophical realism" that "begins from the position that truth can be discovered by the individual through his senses." Both these developments, that of philosophical realism and of the novel form itself, have their origins in Thomas Reid, Locke, and Descartes, whose *Meditations* "did much to bring about the modern assumption whereby *the pursuit of truth is conceived as a wholly individual matter,* logically independent of the tradition of past thought, and indeed as more likely to be arrived at by a departure from it."[10] Here Watt takes us to what is arguably the core of individualism, the fundamental premise upon which it is based: the belief that the pursuit of truth is a wholly individual matter.

Watt's discussion distinguishes itself from others—especially those that take a highly political approach—by placing its emphasis squarely on the individual, absolute reliance on individual perceptions, and the absolute faith in the validity of those perceptions. This is Morris's "psychological experience" in its fully realized form: the perception of distinctness from others, when combined with "a belief in the *value* of human beings in themselves," becomes the conviction that each of us must find his or her own truth.

As important, Watt's characterization takes us beyond the mere self-interestedness (or courageous self-assertion) that individualism can seem to be in political analyses and reveals one of the main reasons why individualism has enjoyed such a venerated place in Western mythology. As an iconoclastic attitude,[11] individualism freed the individual from the constraints of tradition, and as a moral attitude, it based itself, not just on the self-interest of the individual, but on the vital link that it affirmed between the individual, his or her uniqueness, and the moral structure of the universe. By establishing the validity of human perceptions—indeed, the primacy of human perceptions—in determining truth and falsehood, individualism affirmed the accessibility of the moral order to humankind; ideally, at least, it allowed the individual to abandon attachments to external signs and ceremonies and to feel justifiably at home with whatever truth he or she discovers "through his senses."

Watt's insight into the importance of the individualization of truth and truth-seeking also goes a long way toward explaining why strictly political analyses fail to give us a complete picture. If individualism emerges, even only in part, from the individual's growing independence of tradition, and if that independence evolved as a form of liberation from constraints previously placed on individual thought, then it is highly likely that any expression of doubt about individualism's validity would be seen as an attempt to reestablish traditional constraints. The consequent emotional loading would understandably increase the likelihood that any attempt to analyze the issue from the standpoint of what the individual owes to society—or it to the individual—would be adversarial, or advocacy-bound.

For when we speak of individualism, we are not speaking simply about issues of liberty versus social responsibility, we are invoking a belief system, one that, because it was bought so dearly, its subscribers are understandably, and often vehemently, ready to defend against attack. As a belief system, individualism established both the validity of individual perceptions and the degree to which the individual was able to believe in their reliability. If the individual was once oblivious to the possibility of having independent perceptions, Descartes's "Cogito, ergo sum" helped give him (and eventually her) the courage to embark on a personal quest for truth, for which one often paid dearly.[12]

However, contemporary doubts about individualism seem to suggest that, while thought may validate existence, it cannot validate itself: the individual's own perceptions may not provide sufficiently reliable information for the conduct of life. Truth may *not*, in fact, be "a wholly individual matter." Such doubts are bound to be unsettling, for they force the individual to ask, in effect, "I think, therefore I am—but since I am not at all certain about the validity of what I think, how can I be certain about what I am?" As unsettling as such a question may be, it provides us with a clearer characterization of the problem before us. For with this more fully refined focus, a definition of individualism emerges that establishes a good deal more firm ground than our earlier premise that, whatever it is, attitudes toward individualism are changing.

For the purposes of this study, we will consider individualism as *that system of beliefs in which the individual is not only given direct status and value but becomes the final arbiter of truth.*

Perhaps this formulation warrants a bit more discussion about another word: "individuality." Behaviorism notwithstanding, most of us would agree that all of us are endowed with "individuality" because we take the particularity of our individual existences for granted. We see ourselves as individual "personalities" who lived through childhood experiences, "grew up," married, and so forth. We may doubt that we are the same kind of person we once were, or we may, like the Romantics, wonder if we have not lost something in the process of growing up, but we accept that our individuality—whatever it may consist of in the particular—remains a fact of life.

However, the individualistic heritage of the West makes statements such as "we are all individuals" more than a remark about the particularity of human existence; such a statement implies that our individuality, which we take to be a kind of uniqueness, provides the very fiber of our moral character. When we say "we are all individuals," we generally mean as well that, as individuals, each of us is capable of a moral existence. Indeed, when diversity among individuals begins to disappear, we become alarmed, like David Riesman, for we fear that the very core of our moral being may be threatened by excessive uniformity.

The claim to individuality is really a claim that, while animal instincts, environmental imitations, and conditioning may all play a part in one's ability to act and to choose freely, the most critical factor in my own decision-making process is that no one else is who I am; no one else sees things the way I do. As Kant put it, "Persons, because their very nature points them out as ends in themselves . . . must not be used merely as means."[13] When we speak of individuality, we are not generally offering a value-neutral description; we are invoking a belief system that makes our individuality the center of our moral universe. This belief system is individualism.

This book treats individualism as a belief system that makes our individuality the tool for identifying truth and achieving moral worth. At the basis of individualism lies Morris's "psychological experience" of the distinction between beings and the value placed on that distinction.[14] But the catalyst that makes individualism such a philosophical gestalt is the assumption that the individual makes about the nature of truth: that it is accessible to him or her without recourse beyond the confines of the self. This study makes the assumption that the belief in the accessibility of truth to the individual, a revolutionary attitude when it was first advanced, as we shall see, over time became a matter of faith ex cathedra; that faith, however, has been profoundly shaken in the modern era.

Finally, it must be said that this study is meant to be neither a comprehensive, systematic articulation—a "map"—of the labyrinth of meaning implied by individualism nor a definitive, final word on the subject. Clearly, a map of so complex a system of beliefs could be made only on the basis of a particular perspective, such as the one Lukes adopts, and this approach runs the risk of forcing what one might call an Einsteinian phenomenon into Euclidean space.[15] What is attempted here is a discussion of how individualism emerged as a pillar of the Western tradition and how attitudes toward it have, in the last hundred or more years, become increasingly, perhaps even overwhelmingly, skeptical. As such, the discussion is meant only to be a contribution to the larger discussion about individualism, one that is likely to continue for some time to come.

However, this book does attempt something of a reformulation of the discussion by treating individualism from a broadened perspective and, it is to be hoped, with a greater measure of dispassion than is sometimes done. The analysis offered here is meant neither as a celebration of nor as a lament over the decline of individualism. It is simply an attempt to understand the process of decline and to find ways of integrating that understanding into the body of our knowledge about ourselves. Whatever the validity of its findings, if it accomplishes that much, it will have been a success.

2

The Ancient World

Perhaps one of the reasons the genealogy of individualism is treated so spottily is the difficulty one encounters trying to isolate and identify individualism's historical antecedents. What qualifies as interpretable evidence of such antecedents can vary from investigator to investigator, and this fact produces varying degrees of ability or willingness to deal with genealogical questions. Lukes examines little evidence before the Renaissance, Morris all but dismisses the Greeks, and Dumont ignores the ancient Hebrews. Only the *International Encyclopaedia of the Social Sciences* treats both the Greek and Hebrew traditions, but it does so largely in terms of the individual's role in society—the extent to which society gives the individual validity.[1] Investigators shy away from engaging such questions as how and when concepts of the self—perhaps even consciousness itself—emerged, even though answers to these questions are clearly antecedent to the "discovery of the individual" and the evolution of an individualized view of truth such as Watt finds in Descartes.

Individualism presupposes a self that is conscious and able to make decisions about the nature of truth, an "interior" self, and as difficult as it may be to penetrate the more misty regions of ancient history in search of clues to the emergence of the interior of the self, one must at least make the attempt. No one truly interested in the genealogy of individualism can be satisfied with a suggestion like Louis Dumont's that "the sustained exercise of [Greek] rational inquiry . . . must by itself have fostered individualism."[2] For while this remark takes us further back in history than most analyses, a true understanding of individualism will require more than the assumption that it sprang full-blown out of the heads of thoughtful Greeks, no matter how rational they may have been. And since we are dealing, ultimately, with the question of the interior of the self, it may be wiser to take a psychological approach than to adopt the sometimes narrow line offered by logical conjecture based on abstract rational and philosophical constructs. If possible, we ought to begin by asking ourselves how the evolution of something such as the self-concept took place in the ancient Greek and Hebrew traditions.

Eric Fromm's *You Shall Be as Gods* offers us a glimpse of the ancient Hebrew tradition from just such a perspective. A philosophical analysis based on psychological investigation, Fromm's study begins with Freud's assumption that human religion springs from the attempt to satisfy our craving for universal order then goes on to examine the traditions of ancient religions in an attempt to determine which of them most closely approximate the struggles of real life—a feature Fromm believes would encourage psychologically healthy behavior and thus increase the tradition's contribution to humanity's intellectual evolution.

Fromm concludes that the ancient Hebrews established a tradition that fostered a sophisticated understanding of humankind and history, one that allowed the culture to learn and grow from its experience and thus assured not only that the Hebrew tradition would survive but that it would have a lasting place in the development of the Western tradition. As he compares the idol-worshiping cults of the ancient Middle East with the Hebrews and their religion, Fromm makes a remark that bears precisely on the questions we must ask about the emergence of a self-concept in the Hebraic tradition. Commenting on the Hebrew prohibition against idolatry, he says: "In worshiping the idol, man worships himself. But this self is a partial, limited aspect of man: his intelligence, his physical strength, power, fame, and so on. By identifying himself with a partial aspect of himself, man limits himself to this aspect; he loses his totality as a human being and ceases to grow."[3] By contrast, Fromm points out, the ancient Hebrews forbade the fashioning of idols, thereby not only eliminating the possibility of developing a one-sided view of human nature but at the same time allowing themselves to develop an internal, idealized conceptualization of their deity.

In other words, rather than having a group of "graven images" to which they could attribute idealized human characteristics, the ancient Hebrews evolved a unified image with which they could identify and which, since it could not be physically represented, must have by implication resided in the psyche of the individual. This image became the dominant force of their individual existences, however ephemeral its lack of embodiment might have seemed to members of cults who could point to their visible, tangible idols—an internalized standard against which they could measure their own individual behavior.

Two aspects of Fromm's analysis are important for our discussion. First of all, Fromm implies that at a fairly early stage the ancient Hebrews developed the ability to treat idealized conceptualizations as distinct features of the epistemological landscape. We might call this ability a kind of "reification" (though not with the negative connotations that sometimes accompany that word): an idealized deistic figure becomes an internalized abstraction that, though intangible, takes on as much significance as other more tangible aspects of the human experience. This reified, unified conceptualization remains a deity, Yahweh; thus, in itself, it cannot be considered a self-concept. But especially if one accepts Freud and Fromm's belief that deities were nothing more than projections of human idealizations—self-idealizations—the formation of such an abstracted idealization would seem to represent an important step toward the formation of a self-concept.[4]

Second, Fromm suggests an antecedent to the moral imperative accompanying modern individualism. The reification undertaken by the ancient Hebrews was neither arbitrary nor part of a rational exercise. It was embedded within a profoundly felt religious tradition that purported to explain the cosmos and to impute a moral organization to it. The establishment of an idealized abstraction as a deity with significance for the everyday life of the individual was heavily laced with moral overtones: given the Hebrew view of God and history, things could not have happened any other way. Thus the formation of this abstract idealization carried with it a moral imperative. Yahweh was not simply a mirror of human personality; he was also what we would today call a moral conscience as well.[5] We will have more to say about the moral antecedents to modern individualism shortly; however, at this point it should suffice to say that Fromm's analysis seems to suggest that early mental functions that can be linked to a self-concept seem to have been fused with a moral sense.

Fromm's analysis of the ancient Hebrews' "reification" suggests how they developed mental functions that may have formed the foundations for what would eventually be understood as human individuality. But one comes away from his remarks with only tantalizingly scant traces of a self-concept. To establish a more complete picture of how the emergence of a self-concept helped lay the basis for the primacy of the individual, we need a more detailed analysis of the way in which that self-concept emerged. Recently, such an analysis has been made and it bears extended discussion.

In *The Origin of Consciousness in the Breakdown of the Bicameral Mind,* psychologist Julian Jaynes focuses directly on the question of how the evolution of human thought processes in ancient times laid the groundwork for the emergence of a self-concept. Jaynes's ultimate goal is far-reaching: he attempts to demonstrate that Darwinian-style changes in the physiology of the brain were still occurring in the first millennium before Christ and that those changes are reflected in a variety of kinds of surviving evidence, from the evolution of linguistic elements such as self-referring nouns in narratives like the *Iliad* to the transformation of the Hebrew prophets from mouthpieces for God into seekers after a more personal truth. Jaynes's conclusions are provocative and, for some, controversial,[6] but we need not accept or reject his overall hypothesis to be able to benefit from it. For Jaynes's analysis not only provides a wealth of evidence that bears directly on our own topic, he offers a set of conceptual tools that allow us to come to grips with some of its more elusive features.

Jaynes argues that Homo sapiens of the period before the first millennium B.C. was not "conscious," a term Jaynes is careful to qualify. Drawing heavily on psycholinguistic analysis, he says: "Subjective conscious mind is an *analog* of the real world. It is built up with a vocabulary or lexical field whose terms are all metaphors or analogs of behavior in the physical world."[7] Leaving aside the idea of "subjectivity" for a moment, one is struck by the correspondence between Jaynes's characterization of consciousness and the "reification" implied in Fromm's analysis. Furthermore, Jaynes provides us a much higher degree of precision than Fromm does in describing the development of the human self-concept. For the characterization of the individual conscious mind as an "analog" of the real world expresses with much greater specificity the true nature of the abstraction to which we are so tempted to refer in spatial terms, as when we use such phrases as "in the back of my mind." (Such spatialization, Jaynes says, is in fact one of the features of emergent consciousness.) And the characterization of the work of reification done by the conscious mind as the construction of a lexical field allows us a means of identifying that activity within a more structured framework.

From Jaynes's perspective, the ancient Hebrews' creation of an abstracted, idealized deity unrepresented in tangible idol form amounts to the creation of an analog of the real world—a "place" in the mind—which becomes the first step toward consciousness; and the "unified" and very moral nature that Fromm says characterizes the Hebrew tradition is a feature of the lexical field within which this budding consciousness is formed. Again, we are not seeing the emergence of a "self"-consciousness in the highly theistic analog created in the Hebrew mind, thus the need to postpone our discussion of Jaynes's use of the word "subjective" for the present. However, the "unalienated" Hebrew image of God described by Fromm does qualify as an analog that reshapes perception and experience within a lexical field.

Jaynes's work provides us with even more than this very valuable conceptual tool, for it contains a wealth of information about how the individual in ancient cultures came, quite literally, to "see" himself or herself, to gain, not only consciousness, but the beginnings of the prelude to individualism: self-awareness. Taking the *Iliad* as the earliest written document about which we have enough certainty of translation to make inferences about the kind of self-awareness exhibited or absent from an ancient culture, Jaynes points out the striking absence of analog consciousness in the story of Achilles. Scrutinizing the various words in the epic that, in later usage, come to refer in various ways to a "spatialized" self—*thumos, phrēn, noos, psychē,* and others—Jaynes demonstrates that in the *Iliad* each of these had predominantly physiological, not psychological, referents. Whereas traditional interpretations have taken these words to be metaphoric representations of "state of mind," Jaynes demonstrates that a close linguistic analysis belies the metaphoric interpretation. (Metaphor is, in fact, another of the features Jaynes says characterizes the conscious, "analog" mind, and he feels that the "Homeric" mind was not yet capable of metaphorizing.) *Noos,* he argues, is not the sight of "the mind's eye" but a specific perception or a demonstration: "In urging his men into battle, a warrior may say there is no better *noos* than a hand-to-hand battle with the enemy (15:510)"; *phrenes* are "the temporal pattern of sensations associated with respiratory changes [as when we] 'catch our breath' ";[8] and so on.

Traditional interpretations have also tended to see metaphor in the appearances of the gods in Homer, but Jaynes argues that there too we are imposing modern consciousness on ancient, "pre-conscious" evidence. The gods, he insists, were complex sight- and sound-images—virtual hallucinations—that were accompanied by physical sensations in the *thumos,* the *phrenes,* and so forth, and that were generated by one hemisphere of the "bicameral" brain as a kind of protoconsciousness. The gods' appearances provided the motivation for behavior, as demonstrated by Agamemnon's response to Achilles' reminder of the theft of Briseis: "Not I was the cause of this act, but Zeus, and my dark portion, and the Erinyes who walk in Darkness: they it was in the assembly put wild *ate* upon me that day when I arbitrarily took Achilles' prize from him, so what could I do? The Gods always have their way (19:86–90)." Like the Hebrews, the Greeks evoke a mental image—or in this case a variety of mental images—that represent some idealized version of human nature in theized form. Eventually, both physiological words and hallucinated gods become metaphors: in a kind of layering process, a lexical field emerges that allows the Greeks the power of self-reference, and the analog-"I" emerges.[9]

Jaynes does not believe that the shift from an unconscious existence, dominated by images of gods or God, to a conscious existence—the emergence of a lexical field within which it is possible to identify a true analog self—took place suddenly. But for a variety of reasons, he argues, it did take place quickly enough to allow words with predominantly physiological referents in the *Iliad* to begin to have psychological referents in the *Odyssey.* Such words begin to shed their physiological associations in the *Odyssey* and begin to take on metaphoric meanings—many of them acquiring spatial qualities in the process—which suggests that they have become part of a lexical field used to express psychological states.

Phrenes, for instance, which once indicated sensations associated with breathing in the *Iliad,* becomes a location for fears in the *Odyssey,* so that fears of quarrels among the suitors can be put into the *phrenes* of Telemachus (19:10). *Thumos* begins to function almost as a second person within the real person, a "place" wherein recognition occurs; thus it is "the *thumos* of the swineherd that 'commands' him to return to Telemachus (16:466)."[10] *Noos* also becomes like a second person, sometimes nearly taking on the meaning "conscious mind," as when Odysseus entertains thoughts of great cunning in his *noos.*

Jaynes finds other indications of a shift toward analog consciousness

as well: precision and spatialization of time referents and more fre-
quent reference to the future; an increase in the ratio of abstract to
concrete nouns, especially those that, in English translation, end in
"-ness"; and a marked drop in similes. Furthermore, the story of the
Odyssey pivots on the guile and cunning of its hero, qualities that
Jaynes suggests "require the invention of an analog self that can 'do' or
'be' something quite different from what the person actually does or
is."[11]

Jaynes continues tracing the emergence of the analog mind by turning to Hesiod's *Works and Days,* "a detailed personal expression" that
succeeds the "grand impersonal narratives" of earlier, preconscious
times. Here *thumos* continues to have connotations of psychological
spatialization, as does *phrenes; kradiē,* which had heart and heartbeat
associations in the *Iliad,* becomes personified; *noos* actually begins to
take on implications for moral conduct. *Works and Days* is itself
succeeded by the lyrics and elegies of the seventh century B.C. in which
personal expression taking place in time celebrates the differences
ascribable to the individual; "secularization and personalization of
content," Jaynes says, "fairly explodes in midcentury."[12]

But it is to Solon that Jaynes attributes the first real statement of the
subjective conscious mind. Solon uses the word *noos,* which has meant
"perception" in the *Iliad,* far more frequently than anyone before him,
and he does so to indicate a person's inner qualities—what we would
probably call his character—remarking: "Each one of you walks with
the steps of a fox; the *noos* of all of you is *chaunos* [porous, spongy]:
for you look to a man's tongue and rapidly shifting speech, and never to
the deeds he does." According to some, Solon, or at least one of his
contemporaries, delivers the exhortation to "know thyself." The very
concept of knowing oneself, Jaynes points out, requires that one "see
oneself as in an imaginary space," something completely foreign to the
mind of the *Iliad* but something that Solon's particular use of the word
noos and his reification of the term into the imaginary mind-space of
"consciousness" indicates that in the time of Solon the Greeks had
entered "the modern subjective age."[13]

We thus come back to the question of how the word "subjective"
applies to our discussion. Describing the transition from the unconscious, "bicameral" mind to the mind of Solon and the Greek elegies of
the seventh century B.C., Jaynes describes four phases of consciousness
reflected in Greek literature as well as in the cuneiform letters of ancient

Babylon, the Assyrian Gilgamesh epic, and the pictorial representations of several other ancient civilizations. But the special use to which Jaynes puts these stages, one of which he labels "subjective," keeps us from adopting his nomenclature directly.[14] For the purpose of maintaining clarity in our subsequent discussion of the ascendancy of the individual and the emergence of individualism, the word "subjective" will be used, as Jaynes uses it in most situations, largely in the Kantian sense, as of or having to do with the subject as the center of awareness. Taken in this sense, humankind can be said to have entered a "subjective" period in the development of individual self-consciousness when the individual began to develop a lexical field around spatialized self-perception. Where the possibility of having a "self" was once obviated by the individual's immersion in the physiological experiences of existence, subjectivity allowed a "buffer" to develop between the individual and that experience; that buffer was "subjective" awareness, hence its emergence represents a transition from immersion into subjectivity.[15]

We can also, therefore, include the reification of the Hebrews within our notion of subjectivity; for although as seen by Fromm, they may not yet have been capable of the kind of introspection that Jaynes credits to the Greeks of Solon's time, they certainly had made a turn, however subtle, toward acknowledging themselves as the center of awareness. In Jaynes's terms, both the Homeric Greeks and the Mosaic Hebrews have created the "space" that will, in time, grow into subjective consciousness.

With this background in mind, we can turn to Jaynes's assessment of the ancient Hebrews. Jaynes notes a variety of evidence that points to the emergence of subjective consciousness in the Hebrew tradition as it appears in the Old Testament. In a line of argument that, not surprisingly, echoes Fromm's suggestion that the ancient Hebrews took a step forward in the evolution of moral consciousness by discarding visual deistic representations, Jaynes points out the gradual loss of the visual component of the Hebrews' experience of Yahweh, an experience that begins with God's physical presence in the Garden but recedes to symbolic presence in the burning bush and the pillars of smoke and fire and ultimately disappears altogether in such books as Ecclesiastes. Jaynes also suggests that the use of idols by the Hebrews was in fact once common but that in the seventh century B.C.—perhaps not coincidentally at the same time as Greek lyrics and elegies "explode with personalization of content"—King Josiah had the idols collected and destroyed, permanently installing a reified deity.[16]

Jaynes also points to evidence that the analog self is emerging in the Old Testament: the ability to deceive represented by the Fall; the existence of sortilege, which requires a metaphoric capacity of mind if one is to interpret signs into multiple, alternative futures; and puns, which also exist as analogs that provoke divination.[17] But most striking, Jaynes says, is the transition in the Old Testament from early prophets such as Amos, who spontaneously and nonsubjectively deliver messages "heard," much as the Greeks may have heard their gods, to later writers such as the author of Ecclesiastes and Ezra, who study the law and search for wisdom.

Amos, Jaynes says, represents the ancient, nonconscious self, still immersed in experience, without the buffer of an analog self. "In Amos there are no words for mind or think or feel or understand or anything similar whatever; Amos never ponders anything in his heart . . . he does not consciously think before he speaks; in fact, he does not think at all." By contrast, the author of Ecclesiastes "sees" that wisdom excels folly, and he spatializes time and human activity. As Jaynes puts it, he "ponders things as deep in . . . his hypostatic heart as possible; Ecclesiastes thinks, considers, is constantly comparing one thing and another, and making brilliant metaphors as he does so."[18] The late books of the Old Testament, Jaynes concludes, represent the completed transition to the narratizing, spatialized analog self, just as the apparent massacre of prophetizing bands referred to in 1 Kings and the injunction to kill children who engage in prophesying in Zechariah represent the irreversible decision of the Hebrews to abandon all vestiges of direct contact with the deity, entrusting themselves now to the law and their own internalized sense of right behavior.

Jaynes's analysis does not afford us much direct insight into the moral underpinnings of the emergently subjective Hebrews' lexical field. Earlier, he points out that the "beginnings of morality" are indicated by shifts in meaning from the *Iliad* to the *Odyssey,* the former existing in a world where good and evil do not exist, the latter establishing character motives that are characterized as *agathai,* or godly. Although he acknowledges that the consciousness that the Hebrews exhibited as they moved into subjectivity was an overwhelmingly moral one, Jaynes makes no attempt to explain it.

Questions about the emergence of morality among the ancient Greeks and Hebrews probably require a much deeper analysis of the religious and spiritual aspirations of these traditions than I am able to provide here. However, this much is clear from the picture Jaynes paints: since the emergence of the analog-I took place at the expense of features of the ancient mind that had provided motivation and direction, and since the "nonlexical" fields within which those more ancient features existed were deeply rooted in the traditions that had emerged from ancient attempts to come to terms with questions about life and death,[19] then it is only natural that this newly emergent "I" would be fused with those attempts. An "I" that took the place of the voice of God might be a step toward secularization, but it would hardly be a value-neutral development. The emergent "I" would naturally begin to assume responsibility for dealing with the moral matters that were once the domain of gods, prophets, idols, and the like.

Furthermore, as Jaynes points out, a story like that of the Fall in Genesis may itself be an account of the emergence of consciousness.[20] Certainly the development of a spatialized self-concept is a prerequisite for perception of choice; and choice itself is a prerequisite for moral behavior. The story of the Fall may represent, in a much more literal fashion than previously imagined, a recognition on the part of the ancient Hebrews that the emergence into consciousness represented a point of no return that brought with it the knowledge of good and evil.

Briefly, then, Fromm's and Jaynes's analyses of the ancient Hebrews and Greeks suggest several things about the nature of individualism's antecedents in the ancient world.

First, in the earliest beginnings of what we today call the Western tradition, the individual was probably not "conscious" in the sense in which we use the word today: there was no "reified," spatialized self-concept that would allow one to see oneself as an analog-I. The evidence suggests that both the ancient Hebrews and Greeks were deeply immersed in nonsubjective experience until the emergence of this analog-I took place, and because they could not (either figuratively or literally) envision themselves as *having* selves, they remained relatively unreflective, lacking the lexical field that would allow them what we now call introspection.

Second, the emergence of an analog-I seems to be demonstrated by evidence that we have from both the Hebrew and Greek traditions, perhaps over as relatively short a period of time as two or three centuries at the beginning of the first millennium B.C. The trigger mechanism for this emergence is difficult to identify with any certainty: it may have been the profound social upheavals of that period; it may have been shifts in the neurological balance of the "bicameral" brain; it may have been the interaction of these two in combination with a variety of other influences.[21] In any event, the path that led to the emergence of the analog-I can be traced back perhaps as far as the tenth millennium B.C., when archaeological evidence suggests that Mesolithic culture first made dead kings into living gods—clearly an act of analogy.[22]

More important, the emergence of this analog self seems to have occurred in direct proportion to the ancient self's ability to metaphorize. The appearance of metaphor in such documents as the Homeric epics and the Old Testament represents the development of a lexical field within which the analog self can begin to evolve and grow. Metaphor was a first step toward "envisioning" the self, and the self was the ultimate metaphor; with it came subjective consciousness, the ability to see the subject as the center of awareness. Other mental formulations also seem characteristic of emergent selfhood: spatialization of mental processes, increasing reliance on abstract nouns, the ability to deceive, and the tendency to engage in sortilege.

Finally, because the emergence of the analog self was a precondition to the possibility of conscious choice, and because the antecedents of the analog self were themselves deeply rooted in the spiritual and religious traditions with which the ancients tried to explain the cosmos, the birth of the human self-concept was not a value-neutral event. The analog-I served as a buffer between the individual and his or her experience, but it was far more than a structural nuance of cortical organization (though it may have been that as well). The emergence of the analog self was nothing less than the beginning of the tradition of freedom of choice, upon which Western notions of morality and personal responsibility are built,[23] and which generate such tenacious feelings about individual inviolability, as we saw earlier. With the analog self came the ability to narratize, to "see" oneself "in the mind's eye" and to savor the overwhelming enrichment of experience that that ability brought with it. But the emergence of the analog self also created a profound moral imperative for the individual who could now "see" himself or herself. To an ever-increasing degree, as we shall see, the self came to assume the role once played by mental images of gods: that of the seat of motivation and justification for human behavior. Consequently, the enrichment of human experience that a conscious self-concept made possible was accompanied by the grave, even (especially in modern times) isolating, weight of personal responsibility for one's own actions and a diminishing ability to rely on external referents for bearing that responsibility.

Before we leave the emergence of the analog-I in the ancient world behind, it may be worth noting a final correspondence between Jaynes's discussion and an analysis of individualism referred to in chapter 1. As we saw there, Colin Morris feels that the core of individualism is based on "the psychological experience . . . of a clear distinction between my being and that of other people." Jaynes's portrait of an analog self emerging within the individual mind and based on neurological trans- formations in the individual brain might seem to have nothing in common with Morris's description except for one set of remarks, pivotal in their importance but undeveloped by Jaynes in their larger implications.

In a brief section entitled "How Consciousness Began," Jaynes sug- gests that "in the forced violent intermingling of peoples from different nations, different gods, the observation that strangers, even though looking like oneself, spoke differently, had opposite opinions, and behaved differently, might lead to the supposition of something inside of them that was different." Jaynes earlier remarks that ancient traders, far from home, might experience a kind of bicameral cross-talk that would weaken the power of their domestic gods' voices and lead, eventually, to a loosening of the gods' hold on society. "The causes of consciousness are multiple, but at least I do not think it is a coincidence that the key nation [Assyria] in this development [loosening of the relationship between god and individual] should also have been that nation most involved in exchanges of goods with others."[24]

Whether or not the individual first inferred his or her own con- sciousness or that of others, it seems likely that the experience of difference recounted by Jaynes precipitated the recognition of distinc- tion described by Morris and thus greatly accelerated, perhaps even actually provoked, the emergence of the analog self. Such a likelihood is important because it makes even more paradoxical the fact that the development of subjective consciousness produced, in modern times, such a profoundly isolating impact on the individual. And perhaps it may also help us much later when we try to discover ways in which the subjective individualism that is the modern world's heritage can itself emerge from the isolation that its own subjectivity has imposed upon it.

3

Christianity

The fact that Christianity filled a gap in a fragmenting and meaning-poor ancient world has been well documented. Morris, for example, notes that "the growth of great cities and vast areas of imperial government" that took place during the waning years of the first millennium B.C., first under the Greeks, then Alexander, then finally under the Romans, "dissolved many . . . traditional units," such as the family and the city-state.[1] Certainly the tendency is for such social collapse to force the individual back on his or her own resources, the self being a primary mode of survival. But here again, drawing sweeping conclusions from such a tendency does little to help us see more deeply into the genealogy of individualism. Dumont rightly faults those for whom individualism is so taken for granted that "it is commonly seen without more ado as a consequence of the ruin of the Greek *polis* and the unification of the world . . . under Alexander."[2]

What we need is a more detailed understanding of how the shift from the ancient to the Christian worlds modified the self in ways that led to the eventual rise of individualism. And here again, though Jaynes makes only a handful of references to Christianity, his analysis offers us a means for understanding how that transition occurred.

One of the historical developments that Jaynes feels contributed greatly to the emergence of the analog self was the development of writing, which he rightly characterizes as a kind of metaphoric tool,[3] especially the writing down of legal codes. The Code of Hammurabi, for instance, while it helped to keep the civil structure of ancient Babylon stable, externalized and objectified authority: where obedience had once been based entirely on a set of structures that had been so internalized as to be all but automatic, the written code gave "the word of god a *controllable location* rather than a ubiquitous power with immediate obedience." The writing down of the law in the Hebrew tradition had the same effect. The remark in Deuteronomy 34:10 that no prophet after Moses had a face-to-face relationship with Yahweh is, Jaynes says, at least in part a function of the fact that the Law had by then been written down. "The very concept of a cupboard called the ark, for some tablets of written word . . . is illustrative of the same point. . . . What had to be spoken is now silent and carved upon a stone to be taken in visually."[4]

In time, the Law itself became the whole foundation of the Hebraic tradition;[5] it was the objectified externalized form of the more mystical, unutterable Covenant that existed between Abraham and his God. However, by the end of the first millennium B.C., the Law had become calcified; the domination of the scribes and the Pharisees had obscured the personal features of the Covenant, written or unspeakable, and made the deity more remote from the common person in much the same way, according to Luther and Calvin, the Christian God was made more remote by priests and bishops a millennium and a half later.

But the legal tradition that had been thoroughly established as the basis for the religious and cultural life of the Hebrews, both in and outside of Israel, was a further step in the objectification of moral questions, a sophistication and refinement that, by the very level of abstraction it reached, encouraged discussion and disputation, though this was nominally a role reserved for the scribes and Pharisees. When combined with the social strains described by Morris and others, and the calcification of the personal relationship with God, not to mention the influence of Greek rational thought, this inducement to discussion and disputation—"thinking for oneself," we might call it—became much more: it led to a reexamination of the nature of moral behavior that produced a radical restructuring of the epistemological landscape by allowing the self to become the center of the moral universe.

Jaynes does not give a detailed account of how this transition took place, but one summary statement gives us a broad overview.

A full discussion here would specify how the attempted reformation of Judaism by Jesus can be construed as a necessarily new religion for conscious men. Behavior must now be changed from within the new consciousness rather than from Mosaic laws carving behavior from without. Sin and penance are now within conscious desire and conscious contrition, rather than in the external behaviors of the decalogue and the penances of temple sacrifice and community punishment. The divine kingdom to be regained is psychological, not physical. It is metaphorical, not literal. It is "within" not *in extenso.*[6]

The basic pattern suggested here is fairly clear: a religion of "immersion"—the Hebraism of pre-Mosaic times—evolves into a morality of subjective consciousness, first with the writing down of the Law and later with the development of a legal tradition that becomes the substructure of the culture. Eventually that substructure becomes obsolete—perhaps, like the earlier bicameral religions, with help from the profound social changes noted by Morris, Dumont, and McNeill—and a new form emerges, reflecting an even more complex level of analog selfhood.

Louis Dumont places a great deal of emphasis on the world-renunciation features of the emergent Christian tradition (as does Morris) in explaining Christianity's contribution to individualism, arguing, somewhat confusingly, that Christianity's oriental heritage led it to place importance on "outworldly" life (life not of this world) at the expense of "inworldly life" (life of this world), an emphasis that perpetuated individual self-sufficiency. While renunciation, perhaps better understood in psychological terms as delayed gratification, plays a significant role in Christianity, to make it Christianity's primary contribution to individualism is to tell only half the story. For Christianity's emergence as the dominant force in the Western world also, and perhaps even more significantly, involves the further evolution of the analog self— particularly by way of the metaphorization, spatialization, and temporalization it initiates.

The more personal and individual nature of the Christian tradition, when compared with those traditions that preceded, is another well-documented feature of Christianity.[7] But beyond the clearly emergent psychological vision implied by the Gospels,[8] we must recognize that the Christian tradition took new steps in developing characteristics to which Jaynes attributes the emergence of consciousness; thus Christianity itself represents another force in the layering process that ultimately gives us modern consciousness and its individualistic bias.

The faculty of metaphorization, for instance, takes on new proportions in the parables of the Gospels as fictionalized narratives become vehicles by which, not merely the scribes and the Pharisees, but the common person can engage questions of morality through reliance on his or her own imagination. This feature alone might be sufficient to distinguish the Christian tradition as innovative in that it takes the analog self to its next and, for our purposes, most critical step. The emergent self, which freed the individual from immersion in experience, allowed reflection on the question of what he or she might or might not do, but which still relied a great deal on externalized norms (laws) for guidance, is now credited with the power of making its own judgments about the "rightness" or "wrongness" of an action. Christianity does not abolish the written Law, but it does make it a somewhat redundant artifact; true moral behavior in the Gospels springs, not from externalized codes or pronouncements, but from the inherent ability of the self to distinguish right from wrong.

However, Christianity also takes other steps that can be recognized as increasing the magnitude and complexity—and ultimately the emphasis on the self—of the individual's analog lexical field. Spatialization of cosmic proportions takes place in the emergence of "heaven" as a localized metaphor for a psychological state of completion and fulfillment. While other religions may have had rudimentary features of a spatialized afterlife, none made it so pervasively accessible to the common person, or so directly contingent on his or her willingness to cultivate a refined perception of rightness and wrongness—what later Christian theology calls a conscience[9]—and to abide by it. The interiorization of communion with the deity as a substitute for previous physical locations for worship, such as temples, though it does not abandon the "place of worship" altogether, nevertheless further enhances the spatial dimensions of the analog self and, by making that self the vessel of God, spiritualizes it at the same time.[10]

Christianity also enhances the temporalizing features of the analog self, positing not only an afterlife that sandwiches existence between itself and birth, thus emphasizing the brevity of the individual life, but establishing an end to human history itself: the Last Judgment, in which Creation comes to completion and resolves itself into the glorious oblivion of eternity. The Hebraic tradition of history, a succession of events linked genealogically and yoked together under the covenant and the somewhat vague and indeterminate promise of the Messiah, is thus transformed into a rather logical set of sequential phases—Creation-

Covenant-Incarnation/Redemption-Second Coming—which links human history with divine purpose and gives it meaning.[11]

Of course, all of these elements pivot upon a single premise that itself found complete acceptance only after long disagreement and debate: the *homoousios* interpretation of the relation between the Father and the Son—the belief that Jesus himself was fully divine and one with God. Jaynes says:

> At almost the same time that Iamblichus was teaching the induction of gods into statues, or young illiterate katochoi to "participate" in divinity and have a "common energy" with a god, Athanasius, the competitive Bishop of Alexandria, began claiming the same thing for the illiterate Jesus. The Christian Messiah had heretofore been regarded as *like* Yahweh, a demigod perhaps, half human, half divine, reflecting his supposed parentage. But Athanasius persuaded Constantine, his Council of Nicea, and most of Christianity thereafter, that Jesus *participated* in Yahweh, was the *same* substance, the Bicameral Word Made Flesh.[12]

Here again, we see the emergence of a new strata of self: the transcendent. This level is experienced vicariously, no doubt, through the person of Jesus. But nonetheless the analog self comes to credit itself, not only with an innate capacity to distinguish between good and evil, but with the potential for partaking of the divine.

That this potential was established by inference through the example of Jesus—and that it could only be fully realized at the end of personal history—does not take away from the contribution it made to the advancement of analog selfhood. For now consciousness afforded the individual the ability to choose, the ability to distinguish rightness and wrongness, and, by extension, the potential for *increasing* his or her own capacity for communion with the divine.

Seen in a more secular and psychological light, this feature of the Christian tradition is nothing less than an authorization of the analog self to continue its process of expansion and what we might today call "self-realization." For where the emergence of the analog-I in the Homeric and Mosaic traditions seems to have been a rather involuntary extension of the emergent human self, and in the Hebraic legal tradition (and perhaps the Greek rational system) the analog self accepts a somewhat passive responsibility for making choices as a consequence of having externalized and objectified divine codes, in the Christian tradition the self appropriates the power of spiritual initiative. Not only could the individual choose to do good, he or she could choose to become qualitatively and cumulatively *better,* that is, more spiritual and more fully in communion with the divine.[13] Furthermore, the implication of Jesus' psychological logic is very close to that of contemporary therapy; for in the purest Christian tradition one does "the work of the Father" by expanding one's divine potential: one becomes better by realizing more fully one's (spiritual) self.[14]

We are, of course, focusing on kernels of psychological insight that form the pivotal assumptions of Christianity. Early Christianity was no more a religion of pure self-realization than contemporary psychology is a therapy of absolute subjective license. However, the premises upon which the Christian tradition is built, especially when seen within the context of the broad sweep of human psychological history, reveal themselves to be as momentous in the development of the individual's sense of the analog-I of Solon or the writing down of divine law by the Babylonians and the Hebrews. The self as we know it today can be said to have been authorized to make moral judgments by the Christian assumption that the cultivation of the "higher self" with the individual constituted spiritual fulfillment. Given that in the history of the self-concept up until this time, each increase in the dimensions and complexity of the self's lexical field had produced a "higher" self—that is, one in which the impetus toward moral motivation is expressed with a greater degree of psychological complexity and subtlety than the one that preceded it—it is not surprising to find the development of the self a greater and greater focus of attention and initiative.

We see the true impact of the Christian contribution—what Jaynes might call the "authorization of the self"[15] in dramatic form (and perhaps not accidentally, shortly after the victory of the *homoousios* forces at the Council of Nicea) in the writings of Augustine. As John Freccero points out, Augustine's *Confessions* "belongs as much to the twentieth century as it does to the fifth," and in no small part because it implies "the resurrection of the self as author." The *Confessions,* Freccero says, represents the first "literary self-creation of an individual seen as both subject and object."[16] In other words, where the *Iliad* fails to reveal a clearly distinguishable self and the later books of the Old Testament go only as far as meditation on life by an authorial self (as in Ecclesiastes), the *Confessions* "authorizes" a new self, what one might almost call an analog for the analog self: an idealized self that is created as a kind of model for human behavior.

This new authorized self and its creation are indeed deeply embedded within the traditions of early Christianity; they are not the self-creations for self's sake that one finds in modern literature. As Paul Johnson says, Augustine emphasized the dependence of humanity on God, from whom all authorization emanated.[17] But as Freccero points out, many of the "allegories of the self in modern literature . . . borrow the structure of conversion narrative or reveal its impossibility while avoiding its theological theme."[18] Augustine's *Confessions* is not history, it is personal experience, distilled and structured in a fashion that produces reflexive observation and idealization. Augustine the author looks back on Augustine the man, observing how the life of the man led to the emergence of the spiritual self, which Augustine the author now embraces and tries to emulate. Christian self-authorization, in its literary form, becomes the ability to give birth to a new self in a narrative, an activity inconceivable to the mind of the *Iliad* but made possible by the figurative spiritual rebirth preached by Jesus,[19] adopted by Augustine, and used, often to very different ends, by writers of modern fiction.

Furthermore, we can see the moral significance implied by self-authorization ("self-revelation," it might also be called) in the way Augustine's narrative becomes a confession—an expressive act that completes the conversion of the previous self to the spiritualized self—and especially in the idealized nature of this newly created self. According to Freccero, "In a single turning, the reified self led to the self as *sign*." The newly created self is not simply a literary artifice or even an aesthetically pleasing creation: the self as it has been remade in the *Confessions* is a moral touchstone, a signpost along the path to spiritual self-fulfillment. Granted, in institutionalized Christendom, fully complete spiritualization is not gained by the self until death, but the emphasis placed on the process of spiritual self-discovery ("conversion" in early Christianity, "awakening" later), itself an allegorical reenactment of the Incarnation and Redemption, establishes the self firmly in the foreground of the moral landscape. Augustine subtly but perceptibly reveals the inward shift of epistemology provoked by Christianity, and in his creation of a literary self as moral role model he provides not only "the paradigm for all representations of the self in a retrospective literary structure" but the vehicle through which later, more critical attitudes toward moral self-referredness will be expressed.[20]

This discussion of Christianity's contribution to the emergence of a more nearly individualistic self-concept has admittedly ignored one of the aspects of Christian tradition most frequently discussed in analyses of individualism: the importance of the communal tradition, especially in Christianity's earliest days. Morris very rightly recognizes that one reason the early Christians could draw inferences about their own nature from that of Jesus is that the relationship between the Christian and the Christ is not simply an ordinary person-to-person relationship: "The boundaries have been broken. . . . It is not the relationship of two personalities, but the indwelling of one in the other. Since the believer is identified with Christ, he is therefore identified with all other believers."[21] In other words, the fusion of the individual with the Christ not only gives that individual spiritual validity, it also makes him one with all others who have experienced the same fusion.

Morris says that "this element in early Christian thinking severely modifies . . . individualism . . . but it has received relatively little attention in the Western Church."[22] He is certainly right in the latter remark, but we ought to delve a little more deeply into the matter, if only to determine whether or not the potential for "severe modification" may have some influence we have not previously recognized.

To begin with, it is important that we not overemphasize the uniqueness of communal feeling in Christianity. As we have seen, the ancient world was a profoundly communal environment, one in which tribes and nations formed the superstructure of society. The Hebrews themselves, from which Jesus emerged, were so overwhelmingly communal in their attitudes that they were often seen by their contemporaries as cloistered and standoffish—a legacy that still exists today in some subtle forms of anti-Semitism.[23] And since Christianity achieved its popularity in part because the growth of empires began to isolate the individual from some of the communal memberships to which he or she had been accustomed, it should come as no surprise that communality would be one of its recognizable features.

What we should recognize is the fact that this communal feature of the Christian tradition was not particularly innovative; in fact, it can be said to have been at least mildly weaker than earlier communal traditions in that it was counterbalanced by the profoundly innovative attitudes toward the individual that, as we have seen, Christianity introduced. However, if we focus on the way in which this communality fit into the evolution of humankind's self-concept, we discover important undertones that helped, not to restrain the individualistic innovations of Christianity, but to spread them far and wide. As we saw earlier, both Morris and Jaynes feel that the perception of distinction and difference among individuals contributed to the emergence of an awareness of self, and it is probably reasonable to assume that shared communal behavior formed the backdrop against which the facts of distinction and difference could be perceived.

Jaynes says that "bicameral" societies cohered by virtue of their strict adherence to the voice of an authoritative head—eventually in the form of a deity or deities—and that the breakdown of these societies contributed to the emergence of the analog-I. Communal bonds certainly did not cease to exist, but rather they began to lose their overwhelming dominance as the vehicles through which the individual experienced life. But they nonetheless remained the source of many differences and distinctions between peoples in the modern world, and it is likely that such cross-cultural differences were more readily recognizable to the emergent self than such nuances of distinction as "personality." Consequently, it is probably fair to assume that cultures and societies operated as conservative forces—probably in much the same way that Freud describes the formations of groups—emphasizing the differences of distinct peoples and maintaining a substantial distance between them.[24]

Thus it was that the ancient Hebrews were so unique in their insistence that Yahweh was the one and only "true" God. Most societies accepted that other societies had their own gods; they may have tried to eliminate them during periods of conquest, but they never questioned their validity: differences between peoples—and thus between the gods they worshiped—were part of the nature of things. But by insisting that one God stood over all peoples, the Hebrews began the process of eliminating the religious foundation upon which so many—if not all— such differences were based. And Christianity merely took that process one step further.

Rather than limiting the scope of individualization in the Christian tradition, the communion of souls in Christ actually increases it, for it takes away one of the most powerful communal features of the ancient world: the distinction one feels by virtue of the distinct theogony to which one's own group ascribes.[25] With that touchstone for identity removed by the communion of all souls, the potential for individualization increases immeasurably, as does the probability that nuances of individual "personality," rather than social and cultural differences, will become the stuff of which distinctions are made.

Moreover, Christianity goes further by uncharacteristically emphasizing, not only its eagerness to admit anyone into the fold who will accept its fundamental principles, but the responsibility of each member to proselytize and convert nonbelievers.[26] This missionary zeal would have profound consequences, not only for the triumph of Christianity in the West and throughout the world, but for the spread of a more personalized and individualized set of attitudes and practices once Christian principles were transformed into social, political, and economic attitudes.

We may sum up our examination of Christianity's contribution to the self-concept emerging in Western civilization as follows. The externalization of moral codes of behavior represented by the writing down of laws became the basis for the development of a legal tradition among the Hebrews that continued the evolution toward greater reliance on the individual, if only by allowing people access to those moral codes, where they were once reliant on prophets and seers. However, as the scribes and Pharisees took on the mantle of authority by reserving for themselves the right to interpret the Law, that legal tradition itself became calcified and remote from the common person.

This calcification, when combined with the breakdown of social forms such as family and state and the influence of Greek rationalism, gives rise to a radical departure from previous traditions: a religion that establishes the spirituality of the individual self and that self's ability to determine right from wrong. The interiorization of communion with the deity, the localization of such "places" as heaven, and the temporalization of personal and human history with a cosmic continuum all represent, not only a greater emphasis on the inherent moral and spiritual potential of the individual, but an increase in the complexity of the individual's lexical field, especially by virtue of the demands placed on the ability to metaphorize. Furthermore, these features of the Christian tradition, when combined with their implicit recognition of the role of individual initiative in increasing the capacity for communion with the divine, give rise to the possibility of "self-authorization": the development of a "higher" self based on the cultivation of those elements inherent in the self that also partake of the divine.

In other words, the foundation for individualism—the belief that the individual is the final arbiter of truth—is put firmly in place by

Christianity. The emergence of the analog-I traced by Jaynes in the ancient world gives rise to a subsequent discretionary self capable of moral choice; the ability to make moral choices precipitates the externalization of laws in writing, which in and of itself allows the emergence of an individual who will want not only to choose for himself or herself but to find some correspondence between the self that is emerging and the choices that he or she makes.

Christianity provides the basis for finding the correspondence between self and moral order, between the individual and the divine, and in so doing, it establishes the premises upon which individualism can be built. Individuals who can think and choose for themselves and who are convinced of their own spiritual nature—however meager it may appear in relation to the vast divinity that is God—are very likely to take the next, Promethean step and appropriate for themselves their "rightful" place at the center of the moral universe.

4

The Middle Ages and the Renaissance

The temptation to find patterns in history is both tantalizing and risky. On the one hand, it holds out the possibility of discovering grand structures that may explain the human comedy to its participants; on the other hand, it carries with it the danger that such patterns will provide an all too neatly contrived system that smoothes the very rough edges that give history—and life—its color. This discussion makes no claims to discovering such grand patterns. However, one cannot but be struck at the similarities that exist between the period in which Jaynes finds the emergence of the analog-I taking place and the period immediately following the birth of the discretionary, authorized self made possible by Christianity.

The two periods are certainly of a different order: the earlier represents the virtual emergence of the human self-concept; the later represents the evolution of that self-concept into a vessel of moral and spiritual—and, eventually, psychological—self-creation. However, both periods also initiate a process of consolidation and, eventually, codification of the "rules" attendant upon the new order that they have helped to usher in. This latter similarity provides us with the key to understanding how the period from Augustine to Calvin enabled Western civilization to take the final, individualistic step of placing the self at center stage of the moral universe.

Just as the centuries following the emergence of the analog-I had witnessed the gradual externalization into law of patterns of behavior that, according to Jaynes, once were virtually autonomic, so too the centuries following the birth of Christianity represent the externalization of the intuitive truths upon which early Christianity had been based. Christianity's metaphoric features—largely a product of the parables and the figurative speech used by Jesus when he spoke of such things as the "Father" and the "Kingdom of God" and used both for their poetic power and because of their accessibility to the common person—became the basis upon which a grand structure of myth was built that provided the early Christians with a more easily disseminated message, thus ensuring that the innovations of Christianity would spread and take root in a vastly greater area than that in which it began.

That Saul of Tarsus—later Paul—was the chief architect of this process in the early church has been amply discussed, both in terms of the service done to the spread of Christianity and in terms of the disservice done to the poetic purity of its original message.[1] But others as well—Augustine and Athanasius among them—helped to expand upon the teachings of Jesus in such a way that what began as a rather simple, albeit revolutionary, philosophical attitude became a vastly complex, almost labyrinthine, mythology. Rough edges—such as the initial expectation of the early Christians that the Second Coming and the Last Judgment were imminent—were smoothed over through a variety of means, from rational discourse to holy war. The temporalization implied in the promise of the Second Coming was transformed into a much broader vision of cosmic history all but impenetrable to the common person. The psychological interiorization of individual communion with the Deity, while it was not eliminated, gradually became replaced in religious practice with the localization of worship in a templelike "church." Ultimately, what had been a parable-based mysticism became a systematic and institutionalized religion of vast power and influence.[2]

However, we must not lose sight of the fact that, while developments such as these may have diluted the poetic and even the spiritual intensity of Jesus' own vision, they did not eliminate the fundamental transformations that that vision produced in the individual's way of looking at himself or herself. Consolidation and codification were merely tools for eventual proselytization on a scale hitherto unheard of in world history, and that proselytization carried with it seeds that would give rise to individualism in its fullest bloom. The upheavals of the Mediterranean world that accompanied the emergence of the Christian tradition, along with the gradual shift in the locus of Christianity's development from the ancient Mediterranean world to Europe, allowed centuries to pass before more significant signs of Christianity's contribution to the evolution of the self-concept could be seen, but not only did such signs eventually appear, they positioned humankind on the threshold of the age of individualism.

Colin Morris provides a detailed picture of the ways in which the Middle Ages in Europe reflect the emergence of attitudes toward the individual that were made possible by the innovations of Christianity and that led the West to a fully individualistic frame of mind. Morris provides a wide variety of examples of how the Middle Ages reveals a sympathy with individual concerns and attitudes: the growth of references to the self in the writings of the time, the expression of emotion in lyric poetry, the development of a psychological vision, the emergence of autobiography and portraiture, and the use of sermonizing as a means of self-discovery. A look at just a few of these features will give us a sufficient understanding of how the innovations of Christianity became, not simply aspects of philosophy or religion, but features of the social and cultural milieu shared by those who fell heir to the Christian tradition.

Morris notes how a number of philosophers of the Middle Ages reflect the Delphic exhortation "Know thyself." Not surprisingly, the writings of Augustine are the transmission device by which the Middle Ages is able to incorporate a pre-Christian dictum into a Christian theology. "Who is more contemptible than he who scorns a knowledge of himself?" asks John of Salisbury in 1159; echoing him is Aelred of Rievaulx: "How much does a man know, if he does not know himself?" Both mirror Augustine: "[the soul's] God is within . . . she cannot succeed in finding Him, except by passing through herself."[3]

Moreover, such remarks are not mere lofty sentiments expressed in abstract statements; they find their way into the conduct of those who utter them and thereby demonstrate that the individual has begun to come into his and her own during the Middle Ages. The use of personal experience in sermons, for instance, again following the example of Augustine in the *Confessions,* becomes common as preachers try both to explain God's truth to their listeners and at the same time to experience the process of self-revelation referred to in the previous chapter. Guibert of Nogent says: "No preaching seems to me more profitable than that which reveals a man to himself, and replaces in his inner self, that is, in his mind, what has been projected outside; and which convincingly places him, as in a portrait before his own eyes."[4] Here again is the analog of the analog self: the re-created, authorized self that is produced not, as with Augustine, as a single act of self-narratization by which transformation and redemption of personal life is produced but as the consequence of the ongoing, everyday practice of self-analysis and self-revelation. For those such as Guibert, the self is not simply analog-space, as it was for the Hebrews, or even symbol, as it was for Augustine: it is in the earliest stages of becoming an object of everyday scrutiny and re-creation.

That the Middle Ages does not represent the emergence of a fully objectified self is clear from other attitudes of the Middle Ages toward the individual that Morris points out. The lyric poetry of the Middle Ages, for instance, reveals a need for self-expression that is, if anything, intensely subjective in mood and tone.

> The trembling balance of the mind
> Is easily to opposites inclined,
> Love's lechery and modest chastity.
> But I will choose what I see now,
> And so my neck I gladly bow
> To take that most sweet yoke upon me.[5]

This is hardly a Shakespearean attempt to uncover the inner workings of the love-smitten heart; to characterize it as a representation of the modern objective sensibility would be out of the question. Still, notions such as a "tremblingly balanced mind" that is easily swayed by opposites cannot help but call to the mind of the reader the ambivalence, the tension, and the duality of the modern view of the self.

In other poetry the personification of biblical figures, many of whom, as Jaynes demonstrates, lacked what we would today call the characteristics of individual self-conscious personality, is a clear sign of the individualistic bias that was emerging in the Middle Ages. In the place of the brief (and, Jaynes would likely say, very appropriate) expression of personal grief made by David at the death of his friend and ally Jonathan (2 Sam. 1:26), Lawrence of Durham gives a lament that prefigures Romantic expressions of grief at the loss of a friend.

> What shall I do,
> Deprived of such a friend, alone?
> There never shall be afterward his like,
> Nor was there such before. He was my strength,

My rest and my consoling joy. Dear friend,
Part of my soul, I feel my very self
Most bitterly divided in your death.

As Morris says, the striking feature of such poems is "how directly they express the thought of the individual."[6]

Perhaps the two most revealing aspects of the Middle Ages' attitude toward the individual are those that deal with the moral nature of individual life. The Middle Ages witnessed a new emphasis on the importance of self-examination in confession, so great that, as Morris puts it, "the theologians of the age laid stress upon confession, not upon priestly absolution, upon personal sincerity, not upon the hierarchy of the Church. Most of them insisted that the absolution merely proclaimed a forgiveness which God has already bestowed because of the good intention of the sinner." Such an emphasis on the pivotal nature of the individual's own state of mind in the remission of sins is only a shade removed from a de facto assertion of the individual's moral self-sufficiency. Certainly the participation of God in the forgiveness of sin is still absolutely paramount, and the absolution of the priest was preferable—though confession to a layperson was considered acceptable if access to an ordained priest was impossible. However, the assertion of Pope Alexander III that "sin is remitted by contrition of heart" is tantamount to making the individual self-reliant in the matter of spiritual absolution.[7] The duplicity and self-interestedness of which the church would later, in the Reformation, be accused had not yet reached such proportions that external penance was challenged, but certainly the individual who could evoke an attitude of sincere contrition held salvation in his or her own hands.

Morris points out that this emphasis on what we might call contrition of the heart springs from an awareness of the importance of intention in individual conduct. Bernard of Clairvaux felt that "the spiritual life turned on the intention of the believer, for he saw it as an ascent from the love of God for one's own sake to the love of the self for the sake of God." Such a view, combined with the Middle Ages' emphasis on self-knowledge, made a psychological approach to individual behavior imminent. Indeed, while the psychology of the Middle Ages was procrustean and based on the Augustinian "Godward movement of the soul," it was nonetheless another clear sign that the individual was about to come into his or her own as an object of attention.[8]

Moreover, since the emphasis on individual intention clouded the issue of clear-cut good and evil, the self was thus thrown back that much more onto its own devices, and particularly on its own judgment, for making moral decisions.

It would probably not be overstating the case to suggest that these last two features of the Middle Ages' attitude toward the individual's role in moral decision making—the rooting of the absolution of sin in the sincerity of the individual, and the complexity of psychological understanding to allow for the role of individual intention in determining human sinfulness—represent the apotheosis of the truly Christian authorized self. For in the ascription to the individual of both the complexity of spirit implied in what Morris calls "the new psychology" and the capacity (if not the power) for spiritual absolution,[9] the Middle Ages virtually cedes to the individual the power of spiritual renewal and moral discrimination. The individual was therefore as fully authorized as he or she could be within the mythology that had grown up around the simple but profoundly influential teachings of the Jewish carpenter who had set things in motion a millennium earlier. The emergence of a complete and true individualism—the belief that the individual is the final arbiter of all truth—lacked only a secularizing influence, something that would take God out of the picture altogether, or at least make him so remote as to be of little or no consequence in the individual's quest for truth. But before that step would be taken, before the individual set out on the road of fully empowered self-validation, Western civilization seemed to hold a celebration of the individual's coming of age, a period we call the Renaissance.

There are many ways in which to view the Renaissance: as a flowering of the arts; as the birth of the scientific approach; as the return of enlightened thinking after a long night of close-mindedness and superstition; as a period of alternating political acumen and tyranny; even as a prelude to the modern world. Most such views hold elements of truth, but all of them fall into error if they claim the final word on the true significance of the Renaissance. Such is the problem with the most comprehensive discussion of the role of the individual in the Renaissance—or, as its author would have it, the role of the Renaissance in the development of the individual—Jacob Burckhardt's *Civilization of the Renaissance in Italy.*

Work such as that done by Colin Morris and Walter Ulmann has exposed the impossibility of saying today, as Burckhardt did over a century ago, that "in the Middle Ages both sides of human consciousness—that which was turned within and that which was turned without—lay as though dreaming or half awake beneath a common veil. The veil was woven of faith, illusion, and childish prepossession, through which the world and history were seen clad in strange hues. Man was conscious of himself only as a member of a race, people, party, family, or corporation—only through some general category."[10] However, the flaws in Burckhardt's work are largely rhetorical. In trying to isolate and understand the role of the individual in the Renaissance as well as the role of the Renaissance in the development of the individual, Burckhardt—somewhat understandably, given his position as a breaker of new ground—creates artificial categories: the monotonous conformity of the Middle Ages and the brilliant variety of the Renaissance. He engages in thinly disguised disparagement, criticizing the overweening tendencies of the church in the Middle Ages as it opposed individual development. And in painting a portrait of the Renaissance as a time of unbridled individuality, he builds unnecessarily larger-than-life pictures in order to make his point.[11] Yet, if one allows for the rhetorical extremes to which Burckhardt takes his discussion, one still recognizes a reasonably accurate portrait of the brief period during which history allowed the self the opportunity to bask in the light of its accomplishments.

The Renaissance is not properly a unique moment in history. One could rightly characterize the Golden Age of Greece as another such moment, a time during which the consolidation and gestation of the powers of Jaynes's analog-I allowed another moment of celebration, this time of the mere consciousness of existence. The uniqueness of the Renaissance for the purposes of this discussion lies in the fact that it represents the celebration of the *fulfillment* of existence—specifically, the fulfillment of the authorized self made possible by the emergence of Christianity a millennium and a half earlier—and in the way in which it set the stage for modern individualism as we know it.

At the outset we should draw a lesson from the flaws of Burckhardt's discussion as we make our own estimation of the role of the Renaissance in the emergence of individualism. For we have seen that, while there may be thresholds in human development, such as the breakdown of the bicameral mind or the emergence of Christianity, there are rarely clear lines of demarcation that divide absolute categories. Thus it would be a mistake to look for individualism to appear suddenly and strikingly in the Renaissance. What we should look for instead is a continuation of the process initiated by the emergence of Christianity, codified, consolidated, and spread by the early church, and brought to a broad level of development by the Middle Ages. In fact, in the Renaissance we find exactly that.

The Renaissance can be seen as a time during which the authorized self of the Christian tradition realizes its full potential, one consequence of which is a burst of creative energy in art and literature, another an eagerness to explore and discover both the physical world and humankind itself, a third a willingness to tolerate and accept difference and variety of the widest possible kinds. In effect, the authorized self is brought to a fullness of its powers in the Renaissance at the same time that the context from which it emerged—the Christian tradition itself—is at the peak of its power and influence. That tradition shortly became subject to deep rifts that permanently and irreparably changed it and the face of Western civilization. But in the time during which the authorized individual and the tradition from which the individual had sprung enjoyed concurrent dominance, the spectacle of individual achievement is a broad and dizzyingly brilliant one.

Many of the features of the Renaissance that are isolated by Burckhardt parallel those that Morris identifies in the Middle Ages, characterized now by their richness and variety, whereas in the Middle Ages they represent more a promise of what is to come. The portrait of the interior of the self in poetry, for instance, an area in which the Middle Ages demonstrated sometimes unexpected accomplishments, achieves its true flowering in the Renaissance. As Burckhardt says, the poetry of the thirteenth and fourteenth centuries produced "a mass of wonderful divinations and single pictures of the life of the soul"; but the appearance of the *versi scotti,* or blank hendecasyllabic verse, produced a "true and genuine passion . . . a confidence in the power of the inward conception" not possible in the more inflexible Latin forms of the Middle Ages. Later, speaking of Dante's sonnets, Burckhardt says: "Here subjective feeling has a full objective truth and greatness . . . he writes in a thoroughly objective spirit, and betrays the force of his feelings only by some outward fact."[12] The poetry itself bears this out. If we compare the sonnets of Dante to which Burckhardt refers with the lyric poetry of the Middle Ages, or if we expand our notion of the Renaissance to include the works of Shakespeare, the thing we are immediately struck by is the extent to which the interior life of the self is vastly magnified by the Renaissance perspective. It is no exaggeration to say that the original analog-I has become a vast, complex, and rich world unto itself, one that invites exploration and discovery.

Much of the activity that Burckhardt feels is characteristic of the Renaissance's unique approach to the individual occupies itself with this exploration and discovery. Verbal descriptions of individuals, he says, linger over detail with a much greater affection for the specifics of humankind's physical experience. Citing Boccacio's *Ameto,* Burckhardt says: "In his words *la spaziosa e distesa* lies the feeling for the monumental forms which go beyond graceful prettiness; the eyebrows are no longer two bows, as in the Byzantine ideal, but a sweeping wavy line; the nose was probably seen as aquiline; the wide, full breast, the arms of moderate length, the beautiful hand as it lies on the purple mantle—all foretell the sense of beauty of a future time."[13] He then goes on to discuss Firenzuola's lengthy treatise on feminine beauty, itself a compendium of detail about physical appearance.

Physical appearance is not necessarily tied directly to the inner life of the self, unless a preoccupation with it tells us something about the self. Here Morris is instructive, for he points out that "European art in the centuries after the fall of the Roman Empire was more concerned with rank and status than with recording personal features" in portraiture. Morris suggests a number of cases of "personalization" of what had previously been a largely "ideal" art form, concluding that "the twelfth century saw a marked move towards a more individual treatment of the portrait, which began increasingly to display certain details of appearance and personality. In certain circles artists arrived at a genuine personal portraiture."[14]

Here we see the shift from idealized, universal perspective in painting to the earliest form of individualized portraits in which the actual features of the individual took precedence over the representation of an idea. In this, the Renaissance once again continues the shift that began in the Middle Ages and takes it to completion. Burckhardt is surprisingly silent about "the artistic study of the human figure," arguing that it belongs in a history of art, not of civilization,[15] but many others have been eloquent about the Renaissance fascination with the human form, enshrining it as a virtual source of beauty and making it the basis upon which perspective was determined.[16] Where earlier periods had satisfied themselves with highly stylized renderings—often, as Morris points out, rendering a portrait as a manifestation of Christ rather than as a representation of individual appearance—the Renaissance tried boldly both to paint the individual realistically and to make the human body the foundation for aesthetic beauty. In so doing, it openly declared the individual's supremacy.

Like Morris, Burckhardt sees the inclination toward histories of the lives of individuals as another sign of the ascendancy of the individual. But where the Middle Ages produced primarily autobiographies—self-expressions of individuals that were themselves made within the Augustinian model and that made the personal self the subject of the narrative—the Renaissance took the step of producing true biographies: accounts of the life of an individual written by someone else. This had significance in a number of different ways.

First, it objectified the individual even further by making the study of the lives of other selves as valid as the Augustinian style of self-scrutiny through autobiography that had been carried on in the Middle Ages. Second, it served to open another avenue to the exploration of an individual; as Burckhardt says, "the search for the characteristic features of remarkable men was a prevailing tendency. . . . [biography] felt itself free to describe a man if and because he was remarkable."[17] In other words, biography kept the instructive role intended by Augustine and his imitators in the Middle Ages, and at the same time, because it was now possible to study the life of an individual, rather than his or her confessions and self-discoveries, it objectified that life and gave it greater validity as a subject of study: the individual as a complete entity, rather than the process of an individual self-discovery, became the focus of attention.

This objectification of the individual life helps give rise to another feature of the Renaissance that is both identified by Burckhardt and, according to Morris, prefigured in the Middle Ages: the importance of fame to the individual. Though Morris calls it "the author's pride in his works,"[18] the quotation that he takes from a psalter produced at Canterbury and that the designer, Eadwine, placed around a picture of himself speaks for itself: "I am the prince of writers; neither my fame nor my praise will die quickly. . . . Fame proclaims you in your writing for ever, Eadwine, you who are to be seen here in the painting."

Not surprisingly, the elevation of individual lives to the status of objects of study for others in the Renaissance brought with it an increase in the extent to which the individual sought peer recognition. The desire for such recognition is hardly an innovation of the Renaissance. However, when we remember that "fame" in the Christian tradition was confined to being a side effect of moral life and struggle for the honor and glory of God, and that it was rarely something that could be achieved by any but those who were already specially endowed by the circumstances of their birth and their place in society, it is apparent that Renaissance aspirations toward recognition were of a significantly increased order. Thus, Burckhardt points out, Dante "strove for the poet's garland with all the power of his soul"; "the new poet-scholars that arose soon after Dante quickly made themselves masters of this fresh tendency"; and a cult of birthplaces of famous persons, along with their graves, arose. Inevitably, there emerged individuals, like Lorenzino di Medici, driven to extremes; as Machiavelli puts it, "How many who could distinguish themselves by nothing praiseworthy, strove to do so by infamous deeds!"[19]

This willingness to pursue fame even at the expense of risking infamy is a feature of the Renaissance that suggests a great deal about the extent to which its moral fabric was strained by its devotion to the individual. Certainly the Renaissance can be seen as a period in which certain excesses were rampant—ambition, greed, vanity, and political tyranny among them. However, more important for our purposes is to understand whether the Renaissance cult of the individual shifted the moral fulcrum so decisively in favor of the individual as to undermine the very foundations of the institutional Christian moral order upon which it was based.

Burckhardt certainly seems to think so. In his discussion of morality and religion in the Renaissance, Burckhardt paints a picture of moral lassitude and religious decay, citing murder, adultery, vengeance, brigandage, and political license as almost commonplace features of Renaissance life and recounting the corruption of the church, both where its institutional hierarchy was concerned and in the degeneration of the religious practice of its members into reliance on ceremony that often approached, and even embraced, superstition. Burckhardt summarily attributes the decline in morality to "excessive individualism," saying "the fundamental defect of this [Renaissance] character was at the same time a condition of its greatness."[20] But here again, while the broad outlines of Burckhardt's picture may be faithful, the detail lacks precision and accuracy.

It is premature to talk about "individualism" in the Renaissance, if only because, while the individual may, in fact, have appropriated most of the responsibility for moral determinations, that appropriation has not yet taken on any of the systematic form that is necessarily a prerequisite to characterizing it as an "ism." While the Renaissance may have realized the potential for the moral ascendancy of the individual that had been established by the emergence of Christianity, it must be remembered that this potential, even when fully realized, was embedded in a religious system that demanded subscription to its tenets in return for the authorization of the self it made possible.

Even considered in its purely psychological character, Christianity did not extend absolute moral freedom to the individual: it enfranchised the individual as a potentially self-sustaining moral agent under the condition that he or she ascribe to a life coextensive with God, Christ, and the church. Simply put, the core premise of individualism—the belief that the individual is the final arbiter of truth—requires a secularization that, while it may have for all intents and purposes existed for many in the Renaissance, cannot be said to have pervaded the moral landscape. The very superstitions to which the Renaissance was so attracted—not to mention the dependence on sacraments and ceremonies and the outbreaks of religious revivalism so common to the period—make it clear that the Renaissance was far from being the secular age that would be necessary to give rise to a true individualism.

One can say that the Renaissance clearly brought to a high pitch of readiness all the conditions necessary for the process of secularization to begin. It did so by allowing so strong a dedication to the individual that the social, religious, and even moral fabric of civilization was strained to the utmost. However, the fact that the fully authorized individual still leaned heavily on such things as superstition, sacrament, and ceremony suggests that the underlying rationale for a truly subjective individualism was still lacking. The self, even though in full command of its powers, needed the conceptual framework that would provide it, not only with the powers of self-authorization made possible by the Christian tradition, but with true self-enfranchisement. The emergence of that framework was close at hand. But before we examine it, we must consider one final correspondence between Morris's discussion of the Middle Ages and Burckhardt's discussion of the Renaissance.

In opening his discussion of "The Search for the Self" in the Middle Ages, Morris says: "A central problem of medieval philosophy was the relationship of the individual object (*unum singulaire*) with the general or universal class to which it belonged, and humanity was often taken as a test case in this argument." Anselm of Canterbury took a universalist approach to theology, arguing that the universality of human nature allowed Christ's sacrifice on the cross to become applicable to all sinners; but, Morris tells us, "Abelard stood much closer to modern individualism, both in his idea of salvation and in his rejection of general concepts. 'Although people say that Socrates and Plato are one in their humanity, how can that be accepted, when it is obvious that all men are different from each other in matter and form?' " Morris suggests that Abelard's individualistic leanings may have resulted from the fact that "his actual experience of men . . . imposed itself upon his logic"—an alluring conjecture, when we remember Ian Watt's emphasis on "truth to individual experience" as a feature of the eighteenth-century individualistic bias.[21] What is important to note here is the fact that Abelard is emerging from the universalistic tradition, which takes the general class as a representation of the specific object, and moving into what we might call the emergent individualistic tradition: taking the specific object as a representation of the general class.

This is much the same development represented by the emergence of biography in the Renaissance, though in this case ths significance of the universalist/individualist shift is brought into much clearer focus. As we have seen, when the individual is allowed to represent the group—as when the biography of an individual is put forth because it is, in itself, interesting and educative—we objectify the self, and this objectification is in stark contrast to the process of subjectification that has heretofore dominated the emergence of the self. That contrast deserves some attention.

We earlier characterized the period before the emergence of Jaynes's analog-I as one of "immersion"; experience was total and unconscious. With the emergence of the analog-I, subjective consciousness allows the individual to reflect on experience: the self becomes the "place" in which reflection takes place. But such subjective consciousness does not necessarily reflect very extensively on *itself:* whatever similarities they may share, and there are many, Oedipus is not Hamlet; the former's tragedy is a universal and metaphoric search for validation, the latter's is much more personal and existential. In other words, while the subjectively conscious mind may be aware of itself, it need not necessarily make that self-awareness the object of its attention; in fact, it may not pay much attention to itself at all.

Certainly the Gospels do not dwell on the consciousness of con-

sciousness, but Augustine begins to. He creates a self—an act of objectification in and of itself; but he does so within a religious tradition, just
as individuals in the Renaissance exercised their individuality within
the same, albeit declining, tradition. Again, even when seen in a purely
psychological light, Augustine's self-authorization is embedded in a
system that makes consciousness of consciousness (i.e., awareness of
the two "selves," preconfessional and postconfessional) a theological
act. Only the past, preconfessional self is a true object, and objectification of that self takes place because rebirth in Christ enfranchises the
new, postconfessional self and gives it a context within which it can be
objective.

The Renaissance biography very nearly abandons the theological
context of Augustine. While autobiographies such as those written by
Augustine and his Middle Ages imitators were written to educate their
readership, as were many of the biographies of the Renaissance, the
Augustinian autobiography holds up for view a *process* by which an
individual has initiated "the godward movement of the soul." In the
biographies of the Renaissance, it is the individual himself or herself
that is held up to educate the readership. That these individuals were
godly is generally taken for granted, but the fact remains that, as
Burckhardt puts it, "the search for the characteristic features of remarkable men", *not* the process whereby one of them moves toward
God, is the focus of attention.[22]

The religious backdrop against which the Renaissance takes place is,
as we have seen, too strong to allow us to characterize biography as
consciousness of consciousness. But the level of objectification represented by making individuals rather than processes the focus of attention—combined with the fact that Renaissance biography departs
from the subjective confessional of the Augustinian narrative—points
to a development that will have important consequences as the age of
true subjective individualism sets in.

For at the same time that Western civilization seems to be moving
toward a higher and higher degree of subjective individualism, it seems
to develop a parallel tendency toward objectification of the self-consciousness of consciousness. As was mentioned earlier, Shakespeare—a
Renaissance product, but one who arrived upon the scene after the shift
toward secularization of individual life had begun to take place—not
only represents a magnification of the interior life of the self, but his
work reveals the beginnings of a tradition of consciousness of con-

sciousness that will eventually lead to Kant, the Romantics, modern psychology, and the modern, anti-individualistic temperament.

Clearly, this is a potentially confusing development. For if the birth of the analog-I initiated a process whereby subjective consciousness began to evolve and grow, expanding its domain and appropriating to itself the power to make moral judgments, what does the tendency toward objectification spring from? That is a genealogical question potentially more labyrinthine than that of individualism's origins.[23] For now it must suffice to say that the emergence and development of consciousness seems to have taken place along an axis that begins in what we have called "immersion," moves to subjectivity with the emergence of the analog-I, and comes finally to "objectivity." This objectivity is not necessarily the objectivity we denote when we refer to an attitude that ensures greater accuracy (though that may be included), but an attitude whereby subjectivity is relinquished—perhaps "shed" would be a better word—in favor of a conscious awareness of what was previously a primarily subjective experience.[24]

It should be clear to the reader by now that this chapter has presented the long period from the early history of Christianity to the end of the Renaissance—more than a milennium—as a period in which no radical shifts in humankind's self-concept took place. While that claim may seem incredible, it should be remembered that roughly the same length of time passed between the two previous shifts identified in our discussion: the emergence of the analog-I and the enfranchising of the authorized self. While changes of all kinds in the human self-concept may have taken place from the time of Augustine to the time of Michelangelo, radical shifts of the kind identified in the last two chapters did not.

But treatment of this period, and particularly the Middle Ages and the Renaissance, as a single period was necessary for two reasons. First of all, the danger of seeing individualism as a development that somehow springs, Athena-like, from the brilliance of one period requires that the similarities between the two periods be highlighted. We are here dealing with a broad sweep of time in human history, but it is one during which the history of the human self-concept, particularly as it anticipates individualism, is largely one of consolidation, gestation, and fruition of ideas introduced with the beginnings of the Christian tradition. Nothing could be more misleading than Burckhardt's characterization of the Middle Ages as a time in which human consciousness "lay as though dreaming." On the contrary, the Middle Ages was a time in which the first shoots appeared on the tree that would flower in the Renaissance.

Moreover as important as showing the continuity of this period is the necessity of showing how it prepared the way for a new, genuinely radical shift in the way in which individuals saw themselves—a shift that would usher in the age of truly subjective individualism. For the Middle Ages and the Renaissance represent the last time Western civilization would build its epistemological foundations upon institutional Christianity. True, the forces of secularization that the step to self-enfranchisement would unleash took on, at least initially, all the appearances of a religious movement. Many of those appearances linger on today, though they often reveal a gossamer thinness as they try to cloak the modern world against the doubts with which it finds itself beset. But for all that, the great religious upheavals that took place in the sixteenth and seventeenth centuries were to have their greatest impact in the secularization of Western tradition, particularly the individual's view of himself or herself, and that secularization would all but ensure the emergence of the system of beliefs that we know as individualism.

5

The Reformation

In preceding chapters, we have seen how the individual self-concept developed from the analog self—the initial, reified self-concept of which Jaynes speaks—to the authorized self—the self that, through the assumptions implicit in Christianity, is authorized to orient itself toward higher good in the universe and move, however tentatively, toward it. Neither of these stages represents what we can rightly call "individualism," for while both clearly contain the roots of the attitudes that will later become individualism, neither takes the individual all the way in appropriating for himself or herself the absolute determination of truth and falsity, good and evil. That step awaits the emergence of what we might call the "empowered self"; the Reformation makes the emergence of that self possible.

It may seem paradoxical to characterize the Reformation as having established the base upon which Western civilization could build a fully secularized epistemology. How, we may ask ourselves, in the evolution of the self toward a belief that it alone held the ability to arbitrate ultimate questions of truth, did the Reformation allow the individual to shed the belief that truth emanated from some supernatural source? More specifically, how did the Reformation allow us to subjectify fully our moral judgments, empowering the self to do what had once been reserved for the Judeo-Christian God?

One might expect that since, as we have seen in chapter 3, Christianity planted the seed of the belief that human being partook of the divine, the process of secularization involved the flowering of this spiritual seed—the kind of flowering that gives the Renaissance its name, perhaps—and that the self simply moved brightly and confidently into the modern age a fully self-empowered individual. However, we have also seen that the Renaissance did not represent so much a stage of transition as one of consolidation and maturing of the powers of self-authorization that had been born of Christianity; while there were hints of the self-empowerment to come, that self-empowerment did not emerge during the Renaissance. For its part, the Reformation is hardly seen as a moment of "flowering"; indeed, it is often characterized in quite opposite terms.

In his *Escape from Freedom,* Eric Fromm says, "Protestantism . . . taught man to despise and distrust himself and others; it made him a tool instead of an end; it capitulated before secular power and relinquished the principle that secular power is not justified because of its mere existence if it contradicts moral principles." Fromm's analysis of Protestantism is based on his belief that the Reformation was built on a foundation of anxiety and doubt, both of which were produced by the slow dissolution of the social and philosophical structure of society in the Middle Ages in Europe, due largely to the growing importance of "capital, individual economic initiative and competition." While these forces enabled the individual to experience certain kinds of freedom heretofore unavailable, Fromm says that their true significance lay in the fact that they left the individual "overwhelmed with a sense of his individual nothingness and helplessness."[1]

As a consequence, a theology—Protestantism—emerged that answered the needs for greater rootedness and at the same time gave tacit approval to the fundamental social and economic forces that had contributed to our uprooting. Unfortunately, Fromm says, Protestantism responded to the crises of its time in a way that emphasized the pathological, not the liberating, aspects of this dilemma. Rather than relieving the anxieties provoked by social and economic change, Protestantism built on them with doctrines that "taught man that by fully accepting this powerlessness and the evilness of his nature, by considering his whole life an atonement for his sins, by the utmost self-humiliation, and also by unceasing effort, he could overcome his doubt and his anxiety."[2]

Fromm's analysis here, as was the case with his analysis of the ancient Hebrews, is aimed at illuminating a specific aspect of the psychological makeup of contemporary humankind: Fromm wants to coax out features of the Reformation that deepen our understanding of modern existential anxiety. For this reason, he is not the authority on the Reformation that will give us the best understanding of how the emergence of the Protestant tradition contributed to the empowering of the self, though he will be useful in analyzing some of the contemporary consequences of that empowerment. But Fromm does remind us that the Renaissance did not usher in an era of good feeling: the "excesses" into which Burckhardt says the Renaissance degenerated were the beginnings of social upheaval and disjunction that would rip the social, political, and religious fabric of Europe, much as Jaynes suggests the world of the ancient Middle East was torn by upheaval at the time of the emergence of the analog self, and as the Mediterranean world was thrown into chaos at the end of the first century B.C. So it may be wise to expect to find that the emergence of the forces of secularization take place within a context of greater disorder, even of individual helplessness.

Max Weber's classic study *The Protestant Ethic and the Spirit of Capitalism* gives us precisely that context, and it does so in a considerably less rarified fashion than Fromm's. Weber's analysis of the impact of the Reformation differs from Fromm's in several ways, one of which is in the chronological orientation he adopts. Where Fromm begins with the past in order to illuminate the present, Weber takes contemporary realities and tries to trace them back to their antecedents. Specifically, Weber wants to discover the origins of the spirit of Western capitalism, "this sober, bourgeois capitalism with its rational association of free labor," to determine what in Western history provided the foundations upon which the peculiar form of capitalism, "the pursuit of profit by means of continuous, rational, capitalistic enterprise," was built.[3]

That Weber's analysis led him to the works of Luther and Calvin is well known, and we need only say here that the path of that analysis took Weber, by way of Benjamin Franklin, to the fact that the capitalist bias was an "ethos"; that the ethical aspects of capitalism sprang from Luther's "conception of the calling"; and that the fusion of that "calling" with the worldly asceticism of Calvin set the stage for the triumph of the spirit of capitalism in the West.[4] Neither the nature of capitalism as Weber defines it nor the consequences of its emergence for the individual need concern us just yet, for our immediate purpose is to unlock the paradox of why an essentially religious movement allowed the emergence of a secularized self empowered to make its own judgments. But Weber faced a parallel dilemma in his investigation, and his solution holds the key to explaining our own.

Weber was forced to confront the question of how a religion of such profoundly ascetic leanings as Calvinism produced a spirit that liberated such materialistic drives and allowed the individual to take on such apparently unascetic pursuits as "profit, and forever renewed profit." The heart of the paradox lay in the doctrine of predestination, which revolved around the view of the individual as utterly powerless and insignificant in the Divine scheme. "God does not exist for men, but men for the sake of God. . . . Everything else, including the meaning of our individual destiny, is hidden in dark mystery which it would be both impossible to pierce and presumptuous to question. . . . To assume that human merit or guilt play a part in determining this destiny would be to think of God's absolutely free decrees, which have been settled from eternity, as subject to change by human influence, an impossible contradiction."[5]

Over against this view of the insignificance of human efforts was placed a view of a God as utterly and completely remote as the individual was insignificant and powerless; in Calvinism, Weber says, "the Father in heaven of the New Testament, so human and understanding . . . is gone. His place has been taken by a transcendent being, beyond the reach of human understanding, who with His quite incomprehensible decrees has decided the fate of every individual and regulated the tiniest details of the cosmos from eternity."[6] Thus, says Weber, the individual was forced into an "unprecedented inner loneliness" in which no one could help: priest, sacraments, church, even God, for "Christ had died only for the elect." And in the fundamental isolation into which this attitude cast the individual, we can begin to see, not only a mirroring of how the individual must have felt in the growing social upheaval of the time, but the beginning of the answer to the question of how the Reformation produced an empowered self as a response to that upheaval.

For though they are not explicitly contained in the doctrines of individual insignificance and irreversible divine decrees, the implications of these features of the Protestant theology for the individual are clear: God is remote, incomprehensible, and, one must conclude, uninterested in the dilemmas faced in the day-to-day living of human life. It is only a short step from this realization to the position that, if the individual is truly alone, moral and ethical judgments must be made individually, without the sanction of a supernatural power which is indifferent to the individual's circumstances anyway.

But this is a purely inferential argument that we need not make, since Weber's analysis reveals how the leap to self-sustaining moral judgment is eventually built into the framework of Calvinism. As Weber argues, Calvin's followers recognized the fatalistic corner into which Calvin's theology forced believers, and in trying to avoid encouraging a passive, quietistic response among believers, they unwittingly opened the floodgates both to the capitalistic tide that would sweep the West and to the individualistic tide that would accompany it.

Wanting neither to produce a fatalistic Christian nor to frighten the faithful away from the fold altogether, followers of Calvin such as Beza offered interpretations of predestination and of an individual's own ability to understand the ways of God that made practical pastoral work easier and toned down "the suffering caused by the doctrine." On the one hand, it was argued that doubts about one's position as one of the "chosen" were "temptations of the devil, since lack of self-confidence is the result of insufficient faith, hence of imperfect grace." At the same time, worldly activity, which had no inherent value of its own, was seen as a way of dispersing anxiety and establishing one's self-confidence. Furthermore, since "the community of the elect with their God could only take place *and be perceptible to them* in that God worked (*operatur*) through them," good works take on a more substantive role than human powerlessness might at first seem to suggest. As Weber sums it up, "Thus, however useless good works might be as a means of attaining salvation . . . nevertheless, they are indispensable as a sign of election. They are the technical means, not of purchasing salvation, but of getting rid of the fear of damnation."[7]

This is the fundamental link between Protestantism, at least that of Calvin and the Puritans, and capitalism. "Labor," as Weber later says, is "an approved ascetic technique"; "unwillingness to work is symptomatic of the lack of grace"; and, in the end, "the attainment of [wealth] as a fruit of labor in a calling was a sign of God's blessing." Herein, Weber says, lies the powerful logic that would fuel the engines of capitalism and allow secular activity to overwhelm the religious principles upon which that logic was based. "The full economic effect of those great religious movements, whose significance for economic development lay above all in their educative influence, generally came only after the peak of the purely religious enthusiasm was passed. Then the intensity of the search for the Kingdom of God commenced gradually to pass over into sober economic virtue; the religious roots died out slowly, giving way to utilitarian worldliness."[8] This line of analysis is instructive, for it suggests, at least in part, the way in which the Reformation allowed the secularization of moral choice and the empowerment of the self as an independent agent in matters of moral choice.

Taken in modern psychological terms, it is not hard to see the effort that allows the faithful Christian to overcome doubts about election as an act of will, what we might now call self-assertion or even self-affirmation. Although a dilution of Calvin's original doctrine, in which certainty about election was not achieved, but simply existed, Weber points out that followers of Calvin such as Bailey, Baxter, Sedgewick, and Hoornbeek maintained that the individual had "an absolute duty to *attain* certainty of one's own election and justification in the daily struggle of life." While election may not have been attainable, *certainty* of it was; indeed, the individual was virtually instructed that there was a moral duty to *decide* that he or she was one of the elect and to do everything possible to remain self-confident in that decision. In other words, while the doctrines of predestination and election may, as Weber puts it, create "the spiritual aristocracy of the predestined saints of God within the world," one enters into this aristocracy by a personal act of will, and one maintains one's membership simply by doing whatever is necessary to maintain a conviction, like Calvin's, that one is "a chosen agent of the Lord . . . certain of his salvation."[9]

While Calvin and his followers may genuinely have believed that only the truly elect, only those whom God had blessed with a spiritual gift of a genuinely higher order, could maintain the requisite self-confidence in their election, the practical result of the Puritan logic had a more universal effect than that of early Christianity. For the implication of Puritan theology was that only the individual—and by virtue of the resources of his or her own strength of conviction/will/self-assertion—could determine election (again, not "attain" it but, through certainty, effectively make it so). Not even baptism was essential. Furthermore, by seeing the elect as "tools of divine will" and "agents of the Lord" who were thereby justified "in the daily struggle of life," Puritan theology provided a powerful logic that could be put in the service of those less interested in moral behavior than in providing rationalization for their actions.[10]

This matter will concern us later. For now, it is sufficient to recognize that Calvinism's invitation to assert one's own election, coupled with the remote God upon which Calvinistic theology is predicated, was tantamount to giving the self virtual carte blanche in matters of moral and ethical behavior: God was remote and beyond individual comprehension; as a bit player in the dramatic unfolding of divine will, the individual could only assume that he or she was chosen and therefore imbued with all the spiritual acumen allowable to humankind. In the absence of a God who would do so, it was up to the individual alone to assume responsibility for making judgments, as best he or she could, about the nature of truth. And, most important, the individual derived the initiative for taking this bold step from a private, unmediated assertion of his or her own worth.

We are, of course, treating Calvin in a fashion neither he nor his followers would ever have sanctioned, for their theology was just that: an interpretation of the universe built on the premise of divine will. But as Weber notes, the divine element of the Puritan worldview was not one of its most enduring features, and as it waned, the secularization made possible by its logic became more and more pronounced. Weber's emphasis is on the way in which Calvinism allowed subsequent generations "an amazingly good conscience . . . in the acquisition of money," but we can expand that emphasis to include virtually all of human behavior, at least in one specific respect: in essence, Calvinism and the Reformation allowed the individual an amazingly "good" (i.e., reliable, functional, and fully validated) conscience. It may not be that this kind of conscience afforded the individual ease and contentment about his or her lot; in fact, we will see shortly that it did precisely the opposite. But where Weber says that Calvinism "placed the individual entirely on his own responsibility in religious matters," we can broaden the statement.[11] When the religious trappings of the Reformation began to fade, the logic that remained had put the individual entirely on his or her own responsibility in virtually all matters. It *empowered* the self as an independent and self-sufficient moral agent.

This step is a quantum leap from the original assumptions of Christianity, in which, though the individual was afforded the position of partaking of the divine, the ability to make valid judgments was still deeply embedded within a theology that posited an ever-present "Father," to whom the individual constantly referred and deferred. And the magnitude of the leap represented by Calvin is underscored by the appearance of a number of phenomena symptomatic of the pivotal moments in the emergence of the self that we examined earlier.

For one thing, the Reformation produces a telling forward stride in the human faculty of temporalization, one that surpasses the step taken by early Christianity. For time is no longer a feature of the divine plan into which humankind has been placed (see chap. 2 above); time has become something essentially and absolutely secular: time is a commodity. As Weber points out, Calvinist theology appropriates time for individual use—albeit originally in the service of God—and focuses the individual's attention squarely on the necessity of time's appropriate use. "Waste of time is thus the first and in principle the deadliest of sins. . . . Loss of time through sociability, idle talk, luxury . . . is worthy of absolute moral condemnation."[12] As a consequence of Calvin's logic, time became the "property" of the individual, a commodity not only available for use but one that he or she was expected to use responsibly. Stripped of its religious trappings, this attitude would ultimately give rise to Franklin's "time is money," a remark with moral and ethical undertones that exist in a virtually secular context.

This appropriation of time for human use is important in two respects. Not only does it demonstrate how the individual was to treat a notion that had, according to Jaynes, originated as a metaphoric "regionalization" of perception of change,[13] it gives us a clear indication of the character of the transformation the self began to undergo in the Reformation. Where the emergence of the *analog* self allowed the individual to begin to perceive his or her own existence in a self-reflective fashion, and the emergence of the *authorized* self in Christianity allowed one to begin to re-create that self, the emergence of the *empowered* self allowed the individual to become an "agent" fully able to act on things in real, nonmetaphoric space.

Perhaps one of the best illustrations of this empowerment lies in the shifts in attitudes toward the ultimate nonmetaphoric space—land. As Alan Macfarlane points out in *The Origins of English Individualism,* the traditional attitudes toward land that emerged from the Middle Ages in Europe recognized nothing that could be characterized as ownership of land. So indivisible were the land and those who occupied it that the rights of inheritance were not assignable: the land was virtually inseparable from those who lived on—and "off"—it; no one member of a family could claim land rights that superseded those of other family members. Land was part of a domain that fused with the identity of the family and the individuals who were part of both land and family.

But the revolution in attitudes brought on by the Reformation changed all that.[14] Henceforth land was, like time, a commodity to be used to the ends that were determined by the owner. Land was no longer a part of the individual or family, it was a space in which the owner could operate or which could be divested. What Macfarlane calls "the symbolic value" of land evaporates; "alienation" of the land by an individual becomes common practice.[15] Whereas land had once been charged with sacred qualities endowed, albeit through often circuitous rationales, by the Creator, it now becomes a mere commodity at the disposal of the individual owner, whose personal agency becomes greatly magnified as a consequence.

But perhaps the most striking way in which Calvinism affords the individual both a magnification of the dimensions of the self and a qualitative change toward empowerment is in the impact it has on the self's use of metaphor. For here again, where the analog self of the ancient world afforded the individual the ability to metaphorize, and the authorized self of Christianity allowed the individual to use self-metaphor to mold and transform the self, the empowered self produced by the Calvinist/capitalist worldview turned its power of metaphorization outward, using metaphor as a means of agency in the world at large. It did this in primarily two ways—one functional, the other epistemological.

Contrasting the Protestant and Catholic styles, Weber points out that the theology of Catholicism allowed an element of magic—itself, as we shall see in a moment, an important aspect of the power of metaphorization—to relieve individuals from the weight of absolute responsibility for their actions: "To the Catholic, the absolution of his Church was a compensation for his own imperfection. The priest was a magician who performed the miracle of transubstantiation, and who held the key to eternal life in his hand." But "the God of Calvinism demanded of his believers a life of good works combined into a unified system." Throughout his analysis Weber reminds us that capitalism is itself a systematic approach to life, "rational enterprise" built on "rational structures of law and of administration," and in distinct contrast to the "magical and religious forces, and the ethical ideas of duty based upon them" that characterize Catholicism.[16] Clearly, what happens in the transition from the dominance of the Catholic tradition to that of the Protestant is the replacement of all the metaphoric representations, or at least the majority of them, upon which the Catholic tradition was built. In the place of the vast cosmic mythology that had grown out of the metaphoric representations of early Christianity, Protestantism substituted a systematic, rational style of thought that, as we shall see, sought to impose a human order on the universe.

No longer did one see things in terms of the mysterious (and, some would say, exceedingly beautiful and reassuring) cosmology of saints, indulgences, absolution, bodies assumed into heaven, and the Trinity standing watchful over the entire spectacle. The cosmos was now accessible to systematic analysis, even quantification. Weber speaks of the "religious account-books in which sins, temptations and progress made in grace were entered or tabulated" and which allowed the Reformed Christian to feel his or her moral pulse; he also cites the "characteristically tasteless extreme" to which Bunyan carries the idea of God's bookkeeping, "comparing the relation of a sinner to his God with that of customer and shopkeeper. One who has once got into debt may well, by the product of all his virtuous acts, succeed in paying off the accumulated interest but never the principle."[17] Such systematic rationalization is obviously dependent on the power of metaphor, but we must recognize here that the Reformation took a step beyond metaphor—a "magical" mode of explanation that tends to attribute causes to forces beyond human influence—to a rationale, a kind of calculus of human worth, one that has a decisively human stamp. Moreover, this step reflected a new attitude toward reality itself.

In essence the Reformation opens the door to the self's presumed right to impose its perceptions on the world around it. In this regard, Eric Fromm's analysis of Protestantism is very helpful. Fromm compares the logical relation between worldly activity and one's status as a member of God's elect group to compulsive neuroses, saying: "The activity is not meant to create a desired end but serves to indicate whether or not something will occur which has been determined beforehand, independent of one's own activity or control."[18] Fromm goes on to discuss how the search for "signs"—counting of houses or windows along a street, for instance—becomes a means for divining the outcome of an important undertaking, both by compulsives and by normal people in stressful situations. But as Jaynes points out, divination of all kinds—omens, sortilege, augury—are features of the metaphoric faculties in which the individual is able to imagine multiple futures.[19] Fromm would prefer to see this as a neurotic compulsion, but for our purposes we need only recognize it as an enhancement of the metaphoric faculties that have progressively emerged in the self. Powers

that once, according to Jaynes, had been used to *discover* the supernatural order inherent in the universe were now used to *uncover* a
"natural" (i.e., increasingly secular) order in the universe—an order
Fromm and many others would argue is merely imposed by the observer. The self was now "empowered" to uncover its own election, and
it would shortly extend that empowerment, not only to its observations
of the natural world, but to its speculations about the structure of its
own makeup.

Furthermore, the act of will/conviction/self-assertion upon which
certainty of election is "attained" puts a peculiarly modern—and ultimately individualistic—twist on the divinatory powers of metaphorization because it empowers the individual to *bring about* the omens or
signs that portend a fortuitous outcome. The individual is no longer the
passive recipient of signs from the gods that reveal his or her fate, nor
even the devoted solicitor of God's grace, as one might characterize the
individual in the pre-Reformation Christian tradition. On the contrary,
the individual is the agent who determines the outcome in advance
(through his or her act of will/conviction/self-assertion) and then sets
out to produce the appropriate indications that his or her assertion was
valid. Put more baldly, the crasser instincts unlocked by Calvin's logic
would allow anyone to decide on his or her own election by setting out
to obtain the material wealth that, according to Weber, became tantamount to proof of God's favor and thereby established election as a
fact.

This twist of logic is, indeed, nothing less than a tacit declaration of
the validity of human perceptions, the final step toward establishing the
belief that, as Watt puts it, "the pursuit of truth . . . is a wholly individual matter." Clearly, if it is within the individual's power to determine
his or her own moral worth through an act of will/conviction/self-
assertion—"faith," as it came to be known in post-Calvin Christianity—and to produce the signs whereby one's certitude about that worth
is maintained, then the only standards whereby truth can be measured
are personal and individual. Human beings stand alone, possessors of
fully empowered selves, capable of making the most mundane and the
most profound judgments about themselves and their lives, and unhindered by the supernatural "magic" of previous cosmologies. The analog self that Jaynes says emerges as the space in which we picture
ourselves and our lives and that becomes the repository for the Christian mythology that allowed humankind to take the first steps toward

voluntary moral behavior has now shaken off mythology altogether and stands ready to mediate between itself and the world around it.

We must not exaggerate the time frame within which this change takes place. As we have seen, neither the analog self nor the authorized self spring forth in full bloom overnight; while their emergence may seem relatively rapid when looked at within the larger frame of what has gone before and what comes after them, the process of emergence is gradual, and the emergence of the empowered self is no exception. As was pointed out above, the Reformation was, for whatever secularizing influence it may have ultimately had, a religious movement, nor can that religious character be entirely discounted even today, nearly five centuries after it began. In contrast, the main branch of the tree we have been tracing discards the religious aspects of the logic of the Reformation rather quickly, as we shall see in the next chapter. While God continues to serve as a kind of token touchstone for the philosophical discussions that succeed the Reformation, his role can be compared to that of a figurehead monarch: having been relegated to a position of supreme indifference to human affairs, he is himself a matter of relative indifference to those who now argue the affairs of humankind in the parliament of the individual.

However, before we move on to looking at how the self treats its newly found empowerment, we should take note of one final feature of the transition to the state of empowerment on which both Weber and Fromm comment. Citing the passage in Bunyan's *Pilgrim's Progress* in which Christian abandons wife and children in his search for "eternal life," Weber remarks on the "deep spiritual isolation" into which Calvinism forces the faithful.[20] Fromm remarks that the breakdown of the feudal world that the Reformation both capitalized upon and helped to perpetuate left the individual "alone and isolated."[21] These characterizations, while they remind us of the backdrop of personal disorientation and social upheaval against which the Reformation took place, will also become important later, when we begin to analyze the contemporary state of individualism. While isolation, spiritual or otherwise, may not have kept the self from stepping forth and assuming its newly found self-confidence, loneliness and isolation become dominant themes in modern discussions of the self.

Furthermore, as both Fromm and Weber suggest, this isolation virtually dissolved the basis upon which social coherence had existed before the Reformation. Weber says that Calvinism spoke to the issue of community in encouraging "labor in a calling which serves the mundane life of the community" but admits that it reveals a strong tendency "to tear the individual away from the closed ties with which he is bound to this world."[22] Fromm goes much further. He finds in Calvin and Luther an "all-pervading hostility" that is channeled into capitalistic competition and hard work but that ultimately makes individuals strangers to each other.[23]

Both of these features—the burdensome isolation of the self, and the tendencies toward dissolution of social cohesiveness that it perpetuates—become important in the aftermath of the empowerment of the self. Both of them are also central to individualism in the modern world. So it should not surprise us to find that individualism, the foundations of which we now find fully laid, leads ultimately to a confrontation with questions about what the individual's debt to society is and how he or she can relieve the inner isolation and loneliness that empowerment has brought with it.

6

The Age of Individualism

In the Introduction, we have seen that the word "individualism" involves a labyrinth of meaning that is virtually impossible to map with any degree of specificity. In one sense, our inability to do so may spring from the same source as our inability to find adequate generalizations about the larger questions surrounding individualism, its importance in the past, its role in the future, and so on. The problem we face is what Suzanne Langer calls "the obstacle of too much knowledge"—compounded, perhaps by the problem of too little distance.[1]

When we come to the age of individualism, the period during which individualism can be said to have emerged as a genuine system of beliefs upon which Western society began to rely heavily, our sources of information are vastly more rich and more detailed than those with which Jaynes works when he examines the ancient world for evidence of the emergence of the analog-I. While the danger of the latter case lies in the possibility that one will draw too many conclusions from too little evidence, the danger in ours is that in trying to come to grips with a vast and varied array of detailed sources, we may fail to recognize the larger patterns that emerge from the wealth of detail available to us.

To a certain extent, this is the problem with the most ambitious attempt to map individualism—Steven Lukes's *Individualism*. While Lukes does a masterful job of identifying the many ways in which individualism manifests itself in the modern world, his analysis is largely an exercise in what the Renaissance might have called anatomy: his approach produces an itemized list of the kinds of individualism that manifest themselves, along with some of the features of past thought that underlie the emergence of the various "individualisms."[2] However, by attempting to address coherently the wealth of material on individualism that exists from the last three centuries, Lukes's analysis fails to delve very deeply into questions of genealogy and, perhaps as a consequence, seems unable to reassemble individualism's constituent parts into the dynamic, if diverse, force that emerged from the past we have traced here.

So the dilemma we face involves our need to put individualism within a frame of reference as sweeping as Jaynes's analog-I, in which centuries are compressed into historical moments, and our desire to explain and understand as much as possible of the wealth of detail about individualism available to us. This chapter reduces individualism to three primary kinds—possessive individualism, subjective individualism, and romantic individualism—which, if not exhaustive of possible manifestations of individualism of the last three centuries, include the domains in which individualism seems both to have had its greatest significance and to have proven itself most problematic. Whatever limitations this approach may force on the topic, it should become clear shortly that it does so solely with the aim of tracing patterns of larger significance in a landscape crowded with interrelated detail.

Possessive Individualism

Possessive individualism is the manifestation of individualism that has been most thoroughly discussed by recent scholarship in one form or another, perhaps because it lies at the heart of liberal-democratic ideas about individualism that are commonly analyzed from the perspective of political philosophy.[3] One author, C. B. Macpherson, has written a thorough analysis of possessive individualism to which we will turn in a moment. However, we should first make clear the historical antecedents of possessive individualism.

We have seen that Calvinism afforded individuals the ability, in effect, to interpret personal experience selectively in such a way as to reassure themselves of their spiritual integrity. One could *"attain* certainty of [one's] own individuality and justification in the daily struggle of life" simply by finding evidence that satisfactorily demonstrated the certainty of election.[4] Such confirmation of certainty was obtained within the frame of reference that Calvinist logic provided, and as Weber demonstrates, that logic bore a powerful affinity with economic matters.

Though Calvin never intended it as such, Calvinistic logic effectively allowed economic success to become a sign—perhaps even *the* sign— by which the faithful could identify election. And since such signs were, as we have seen, really acts of will/conviction/self-assertion, the economic domain very quickly became one of the primary domains in which the newly empowered self came to operate.[5] As the religious trappings of Calvinistic logic were shed, the empowered self began to test and expand its powers in terms of the individual's ability to acquire and possess. Where the self had, since the time of Christ, rooted itself within the framework of Christian theology and cosmology, what we have called its "empowerment" also brought an entirely new context that replaced the framework of Christianity with the framework of possessive capitalism.

In his discussion of possessive individualism, Macpherson is even less interested in genealogy than Lukes, but his very comprehensive study of how economic assumptions create the substructure upon which post-Calvinistic philosophy is built gives us a picture of the consequences of the Calvinistic revolution for the individual's self-image. Summing up the "assumptions which comprise possessive individualism," Macpherson says that seventeenth-century philosophy provided the basis for an economically based individualism by affirming that "what makes a man human is freedom from dependence on the will of others" and by seeing the significance of this feature of human nature primarily in terms of *proprietorship*. Tracing this attitude to Hobbes, Macpherson says that "the human essence" becomes reduced to "freedom from others' wills and proprietorship of one's own capacities."[6] The connection with Calvinism is clear: the individual is no longer either a "tool of the gods," as in the Greek tradition, a "chosen one of God," as in the Hebrew, or even a "child of God," as in the Christian. The empowering of the self makes the individual a "free man," but it does so largely with respect to the individual's position as an "owner" of himself or herself.[7]

It is from this basic premise of "self-possession" that, according to Macpherson, all of the tenets of possessive individualism—and, ultimately, liberal democracy—spring. Once he or she is established as what we might call a free agent, the individual's freedom "can rightfully be limited only by such obligations . . . necessary to secure the same freedom for others"; the political foundations upon which society are built are nothing more than "a contrivance for the protection of the individual's property *in his person and goods,* and (therefore) for the maintenance of orderly relations of exchange between individuals regarded as *proprietors of themselves*." The consequences of the Calvinistic revolution, both in the form that Hobbes gave them and in the variously elaborated and emended version put forth by the Puritan Levellers, James Harrington and John Locke, are readily apparent in this premise, which arranges human nature and human freedom in a pattern from which possessive individualism is woven.[8] Moreover, one can see plainly the way in which the woof is immediately drawn across this warp in such a fashion that the design will take on the political character that so much discussion of individualism adopted. As Macpherson and others point out, the premise of self-ownership—itself a clear and very powerful implication of the emergence of the empowered self—combined with the ability afforded that self by Calvinism to find its own "signs" in the material world, rather than the spiritual world, leads directly into the evolution of liberal-democratic theory.

Lukes provides a discussion of the emergence of the liberal-democratic tradition from the political assumption of the seventeenth century, though he unfortunately only compares the features of what he calls "political individualism" and "economic individualism" without demonstrating how one follows from the other.[9] The question of how one is to reconcile the freedom of individual selves with the points at which such individual freedoms overlap and, inevitably, conflict is one of the most common themes running through political philosophy from the time of Hobbes to the present. It also has implications, as we shall see later, for aspects of subjective individualism and romantic individualism.

However, for reasons that should by now be apparent, this study does not take possessive individualism, or the questions of political philosophy it raises, to be the most significant feature of the individualistic matrix of beliefs that begins to emerge as a consequence of the Calvinistic revolution. Possessive individualism is significant in three respects.

First, it represents the tangible consequence of Calvinism's emphasis on the material world as the medium through which the all-important signs of election were to be discovered. That emphasis on the material world was a major contribution to the emergence of scientific inquiry and to the organization of scientific knowledge in a systematic fashion, both of which have had a profound impact on the degree to which the economic and political consequences of possessive individualism could take root and flourish.

Second, it provides a domain in which the empowered self could test its powers. As we saw in the last chapter, this domain is parallel to the metaphors of space that Jaynes finds in the emergence of the analog-I in the ancient world, but with the now fully empowered self exercising its empowerment in literal, rather than figurative, space. Where previously the self had measured itself, at least in part, by the interior regions that its experience of Greek self-knowledge, Judaic law, and Christian cosmology allowed it, now the logic of Calvinism allowed the self to measure itself by its exercise of initiative in the more and more literal space represented by ownership. Already, the Renaissance fascination with exploration and discovery had led the individual to reconceptualize the shape of physical space and to explore the new globe that emerged; eventually, the transformation of space into a domain in which the empowered self could test and prove itself would give rise to the quest for *proprietorship* of that same global space, a quest we have come to call capitalism.

Finally, possessive individualism provides the basis upon which some of the most apparent and powerful challenges to the assumptions of individualism could be made: the conflicts that must inevitably emerge out of the attempts by an unlimited number of individuals of unequal talents and position, operating within an increasingly finite economic "space" to achieve and enjoy the benefits of proprietorship, would raise profound, perhaps even unanswerable questions about the viability of the liberal-democratic theories that had been built upon the premises of possessive individualism.[10]

However, for all its significance, possessive individualism is not the most important feature of the individualistic system of beliefs that began to dominate the Western world after the Reformation. For the very "materialistic" foundation upon which possessive individualism was, at least in part, based gave it problems, and the attempts to come to terms with those problems opened up a new and potentially much more vast domain in which the self was free to explore, though, as we shall see, this domain offered a considerably less concrete set of standards by which the empowered self could test and prove itself.

Subjective Individualism

While the Calvinistic act of conviction/will/self-assertion that led the newly empowered self to search for signs in the economic domain guaranteed that much of the life of the self would be concerned with the material world and, specifically, property, we must recognize that the interior life of the self was not abandoned with the onset of the age of capitalism. On the contrary, a preoccupation with the interior features of consciousness continues well into the development of Western capitalism; in fact, it intensifies the development of individualism itself and, ultimately, helps to make it so problematic. This preoccupation seems, perhaps not surprisingly, to go briefly into eclipse in the years immediately after the Reformation as the empowered self steps out to take its place in the proprietary world of Hobbes and Locke. However, the nature of the material world itself soon becomes the focus of intense speculation and doubt, and the self is eventually led back to a direct confrontation with the limits of its own powers.

Initially, the empowered self's new sense of proprietorship over the material world that it inhabited merged with the scientific approach, which had begun to flower in the Renaissance in an attempt to map the physical world that now seemed humankind's rightful inheritance.[11] In this endeavor, Western thought was not yet ready to abandon the notion that some divine influence held sway in the organization of the universe. While not necessarily subscribing to the circularity of method that characterized religiously acceptable "scientific" explanations of the past, the newly empowered self did make the somewhat circular assumption that the universe must be based on reasonable principles of organization and that such organization would eventually yield itself to the powers of reasonable scrutiny, allowing a fusion of cosmic and human reason to take place.

This belief had its origins in what Paul Johnson calls "the third force" of Christianity, a group of enlightened thinkers who hoped for reconciliation between the forces of Reformation and counter-Reformation in the sixteenth century. According to Johnson, this group held "to the belief, quite common among sixteenth-century intellectuals, that there was a complete and final system of knowledge to be discovered, which embraced all the arts and sciences, and revolved around Christianity. When, in due course, this system was completely unveiled, it would automatically solve all religious disputes and controversies."[12] The hope for religious reconciliation faded, but the idea of a unified universe persisted, ultimately finding its expression in the philosophies of Leibnitz, the early Voltaire, Descartes, Bacon, Pope, and even, to some extent, Hobbes and Locke. This was the philosophy of "the best of all possible worlds," which was so profoundly shaken by the Lisbon earthquake.

One might think of this philosophy as another "projection" of the kinds that Eric Fromm attributes to both the ancient Hebrews and the heirs to Calvinistic logic: the empowered self, having finally come into its own, mistakenly attributed its own powers of reason to the world it inhabited, and only with the intervention of an event that demonstrated the less-than-reasonable nature of the universe was it forced to admit its error. However, the Lisbon earthquake, while it shook the philosophical presuppositions of thinkers like Voltaire very deeply, could not alone have accounted for the collapse of so fundamental an attitude as the expectation that the universe would conform to the "reasonable" expectations of humankind. For with the development of a scientific approach, which lay beneath attempts to discover the blueprint behind the clockwork universe, Western thought shed the religious trappings from which that approach had emerged, just as it had shed the religious trappings of attitudes about property, and in the process subjective individualism was established as the dominant moral, philosophical, and metaphysical attitude of the age.

In the face of the universe's unwillingness to conform to the individual's expectations of it, the empowered self had really only one choice: to turn inward and to examine itself and the degree to which it was capable of knowing. David Hume helped to begin this process in earnest with his "critical philosophy," in which he refused to take anything on faith and remained skeptical about any assertion of truth that was not based on empirical evidence. No one could begin with the assumption that the universe had a reasonable organization, Hume said, because any attempt to do so would violate the empirical method. Everything must be subjected to what Watt has termed "the study of the particulars of experience by the individual investigator who, ideally at least, is free from the body of past assumptions and traditional beliefs,"[13] and the assumption of an ordered and reasonable universe violated that principle. True to the tradition of the newly empowered self, Hume insisted that investigation of the reality inhabited by the individual must begin fresh and free from presuppositions, theistic or otherwise.

But Hume's empiricism took him a step further than mere critical skepticism. In examining the relationship between what we perceive and what is actually there, he naturally refused to consider the possibility that the individual is an exception to the exclusion of a priori truths. So Hume threw out the notion that we are somehow imbued with innate ideas that help us to sort out the reality we inhabit. Human knowledge, he argued, is nothing more than an accumulated buildup of impressions from experience that crystallize in the mind of the individual as ideas. Ultimately, we must even be skeptical about our own existences and that of the external world we inhabit, simply because we have nothing against which to test the validity of either but our minds, which are suspect by virtue of the fact that they are subjective.

The blow Hume struck for individualism was profound, for his position completely eliminated, once and for all, the possibility that human existence came with any supernatural guarantees of certainty, at least of the kind the "authorized" self had been led to expect. Though attempts to reinstate such certainties would be made by such thinkers as Kant and Hegel, they would never have the force that they had in pre-Reformation times. The individual self reached the stage at which its empowerment could be said to be complete: individuals were now on their own and had to assume all the freedom and all the responsibility that came with that position.

It is interesting to note both what the individual did with that freedom and how, in some cases, attempts were made to avoid that responsibility. For while Hume may have severely limited the degree to which the empowered self could gain certainty about anything, he did not diminish its desire to inquire and explore. Hume's conclusions further intensified the reflexive nature of epistemological inquiry, focusing attention more acutely on this entity, the self, which had apparently been proven so paralyzed in its drive to satisfy its curiosity and attain some degree of certainty.

We can see a double action taking place here. In one respect, the empowered self can be said to be searching for some way out of the canyon into which Hume had taken it, trying to find the means by which it could establish the validity of its own perceptions. But the attempt to do so required an even closer scrutiny of the self itself. Any demonstration that the individual *could* know would require a more careful, detailed, and specific analysis of the self, and this analysis itself began, as we shall see, to take on a life of its own.

Immanuel Kant might in some respects be characterized as one of the fathers of modern psychology. But Kant's aims in such works as the *Critique of Pure Reason* were not, strictly speaking, psychological.

Trained in the Leibnitzian worldview of an ordered universe governed by a priori principles, Kant was "awakened from his dogmatic slumber" by Hume's *Enquiry concerning Human Understanding* and its insistence on "critical philosophy."[14] Kant did not, like Hume, debunk metaphysics altogether; he believed, as we shall see, that we could achieve some certainty about ourselves and our world. But Kant was deeply sympathetic to Hume's insistence on the testability of assertions about humankind, the universe, and the relationship between them.

It is not the purpose of this discussion to provide a coherent recounting, even of the most cursory kind, of Kant's philosophy. However, in order to understand the importance of what Lukes calls "epistemological individualism"[15]—indeed, its pivotal position in the genealogy of individualism—it is necessary to discuss several features of Kant's metaphysics, especially as they relate to the individual, individual perceptions, and how those perceptions begin to allow a detailed picture to emerge of what we today call the human psyche.

To begin with, Kant divides what is "not self" into two realms: the world, which we apprehend with our common, everyday sense perceptions; and reality, which lies behind the appearances that present themselves in those common, everyday sense perceptions. The real difference between the world as we perceive it and reality is that, in the act of perception, we reorganize reality and give it a form in time and space that makes it accessible to us. This accessible, organized world is the world of "phenomena." Having established the difference between perceived phenomena and reality, Kant begins to examine the ways in which we organize reality to make it accessible. Not only do we contribute forms in space and time, Kant says, we categorize "noumena" (phenomena before they are organized) in a way that gives structure and coherence to all that we perceive. These categories include such things as quality, quantity, relation, and modality (degree of possibility, actuality, or necessity); not only are they the basis upon which we perceive and understand the reality we inhabit, but *they reveal the structure of the very understanding with which we apprehend that reality.*

Neither the division of the nonself into noumena and phenomena nor the categories Kant proposes (which are themselves taken from traditional logic) are as important for our purposes as this last assertion that our understanding reveals itself in the *way* in which it operates. For with this assertion—itself an attempt to delineate the nature of human

understanding with greater specificity so that the validity of its perceptions can be established—Kant trains the focus of the discussion on
what, rather than *whether,* the self is, and though he does not end the
discussion of whether the self can know anything, he opens the door to
the whole range of modern psychological inquiry: speculation about
the self by the self. Such inquiry, by its very existence, asserts an
affirmative answer to the question of "whether" and at the same time
helps to establish an entirely new, individualistic field parallel to, but
far more complex than, the "lexical" field that Jaynes attributes to the
analog-I of the ancient world.

Indeed, Kant and the modern psychological theories to which he
opened the door firmly entrench the empowered self in an existence
free from the a priori moral and cosmological beliefs that had hitherto
given shape to all human perceptions. By asserting that we ourselves
give shape to reality by perceiving it, Kant establishes at the fundamental level of metaphysics what Watt says Descartes did much to bring
about: "the assumption whereby the pursuit of truth is conceived of as
a wholly individual matter." Furthermore, the demonstration of the
"structure" of understanding that Kant makes on the basis of the way
in which we perceive becomes (again, perhaps unwittingly, as with
Calvin's search for signs of election) a tacit acknowledgment of the
primacy of the self in that it allows a shift away from the question of the
validity of perceptions to the nature and structure of those perceptions
and of the perceiving agent. That shift is of great importance because,
in effect, it authorizes deep probing of the nature of the self and psyche,
probing that in itself can be seen as a final product of individualism.

However, before we examine the arguably more "objective" field
represented by modern psychology, we should continue to trace the
path of subjective individualism as represented by Kant. For Kant was
not content to let a more detailed analysis of the faculties of human
understanding stand as an assertion that human understanding had validity. He wanted to establish a firm bridge between perceived phenomena and the noumena that made up reality, and in so doing he helped to
create the momentum that would produce romantic individualism.

In his search for a link between human perception and reality, Kant
struck upon two notions. First, he decided that, since human perception was a product of reality, it must also be a kind of mirror for reality,
revealing information about the noumenal world just as it did information about itself. As Morse Peckham puts it, "Since . . . the mind ex-

hibits a purposive drive toward organization . . . it seems reasonable and indeed necessary to assume—though it can never be proved—that because the mind is after all a product of reality, reality itself is informed by a purposive organizing drive. Not in its structure but in its drive toward structure is the mind analogous to reality."[16] In other words, while the structure of human understanding and that of nature might be distinct from one another, the motivating force behind them was similar and might even be the same.

Second, in order to explain how individuals could recognize this similarity, even harmonize themselves with it, Kant postulated the existence of two kinds of will: that of the inner self—the "autonomous" will, and that of the external principle—the "heteronymous" will. The first of these reflects the will of the "noumenal" self, or true self, unhindered by desires or practical considerations, responding only to such things as "duty" and "respect"; as such, it represents human beings at their most genuine, in their capacity to break through the appearances of the phenomenal and come into contact with the noumenal world of reality. Kant felt that this ability to see through phenomenal appearances held the key to bridging the gap between humankind and reality, and it exercised itself most completely under the influence of what Kant called the categorical imperative.

The categorical imperative was quite simply the intuitive knowledge of truth inherent in every individual, a knowledge free from desires and needs, skills or selfish ends, which affords each individual the opportunity (not the necessity, however) of acting in accordance with the noumenal world. Herein lay what Hume had failed to find: a feature of human understanding that reestablished, not only the ability of the individual to perceive reality, but also the ability to act in accordance with that reality. Whether or not this feature of human understanding met Hume's empirical criteria is questionable, and Kant's assertion that one could penetrate through the world of appearances and come into contact with reality has been a matter of controversy ever since he made it. But here again, we need neither agree nor disagree to be able to weigh the significance of Kant's ideas in the course followed by, and greatly influenced by, subjective individualism. Along with the practical imperative—the inherent sense we all have, responded to or not, that every individual must be perceived as an end in himself or herself rather than as a means—the existence of the categorical imperative establishes the moral basis for individual action in a highly secularized, metaphysical context. Kant was not himself religious; though he believed in a divine order, his philosophy was so heavily predicated on the metaphysics of the individual encounter with reality that it emerges as a de facto validation of the individual's moral capability without reference to God.

Perhaps even more important, Kant's emphasis on the individual's ability to come into contact with reality through action—action based on the "autonomous" will responding to the categorical imperative—reinstalled the individual as an agent for whom independent moral judgment was not only possible but natural and for whom action was a kind of moral litmus test. In effect, Kant installed the autonomous individual as the moral center of the universe capable of affecting a deeply resonant union with that universe. Quite simply, Kant made possible the third brand of individualism we will look at: romantic individualism.

But before we look at how individualism fared in the hands of the Romantics, we should take a close look at the way in which Kant's focus on the structure of human understanding represents both a shift in attitude toward the self and an expansion of the human conception of the self.

We have seen that, by taking the discussion beyond Hume's doubts about the validity of human understanding, Kant allowed a de facto validation to take place. Though he used such concepts as the autonomous will and the categorical imperative to support his own conviction that human understanding was valid, his turn toward analyzing the *structure* of that understanding was in fact a digression of such compelling interest that the original investigation lost some of its attraction. However, to characterize this shift as a mere digression would be to miss the point of what Kant really achieves. In focusing on structure, Kant opens the door to a deeper probing of the nature of the self than previously possible. In effect, he does for the self what Calvinistic logic did for the material world: he allows *it* to become a domain in which to test the individual's powers, now of reflection, where the material world tested the individual's powers of production.

In other words, though in the *Critique of Pure Reason* he calls the intuition of an "objective" self a mistaken apprehension, Kant helps to reestablish "interior" space as one of the domains in which the individual operates. The shift of emphasis to external signs as a validation of self-worth made possible by Calvinism and possessive individualism had temporarily undercut the role of the interior self, but Hume's doubts about human perception—which naturally brought the perceived material world itself into question—began the process of re-establishing the pivotal nature of the interior self, and Kant's analysis of its structure completed it. For our purposes, it is important to recognize the ways in which the "new" interior domain made possible by Kant differed from what had gone before; for in analyzing "human understanding," Kant is really dealing with *processes* that take place within the mind-space Jaynes says emerged with the analog-I.

To begin with, we are clearly dealing with a full secularized self in Kant. God, as we have said, plays only the remotest of roles and could be removed without affecting the whole in any appreciable way; the interior mind-space in Kant is, for all intents and purposes, godless in any Christian sense. But the interior self is also, by definition, the seat of moral agency. While one may be able to exclude an authorizing Christian God from Kant's world view without radically altering it, there is no avoiding the conclusion that Kant saw the individual as a being capable of, though not necessarily required to engage in, moral behavior. And the touchstone for that moral behavior, the categorical imperative, existed in the self as an inherent part of human understanding. In other words, the self's moral empowerment was a given in the basic equation of human existence.

Second, Kant's mind-space is far more literal—and far more concerned with objectivity—than it is figurative; it is expressed far less imagistically than the mind-space of the Greek, Hebrew, or Christian worldview. Where the analog self is expressed in forms that represent a slight advance over similes—what Jaynes calls "preconscious hypostases"—and the authorized self is expressed in the vast Christian cosmology of Trinity, eternity, and paradise, Kant's analysis is expressed in terms one might expect of a scientific grid—"categories," as he calls them. To be sure, Kant's analysis is highly abstract; but in abstracting, he does not lean on imagery. His is the classical philosophical treatise of dense phrasing and abstraction that takes language to its limits and beyond.

For the third and most important feature of the mind-space reflected in Kant is linguistic, and it requires us to backtrack somewhat. Jaynes argues that the ancient world witnessed emergence of a lexical field that allowed humankind to begin talking about experience in "analog" terms: when, for instance, we say, "I felt afraid," we are positing an analog self—the "I"—whom we were at the time we felt fear but no longer are. As this field or network of meaning expanded, Jaynes says, members of ancient civilizations came to "see" themselves as having a whole range of features "located" within this mind-space. Eventually, the mind-space took on a life of its own as words allowing temporalization and spatialization emerged into common usage. This is the period of the analog-I.

In the period of what we have called the "authorized" self, there is an expansion of the domain of the mind-space of such magnitude that we might say that the lexical field of the analog-I has become a "grammatical" field. For now not only are there, by comparison with the period of the analog self, a vast range of words that can be used to refer to the mind-space, they have taken on functions that go beyond simple description and begin to articulate qualitative transformations in aspects of consciousness.[17] For instance, in a somewhat oversimplified interpretation of Christian terms based on modern psychology, one might characterize the state of "grace" as a state of psychological well-being, balance, and fullness, while a state of "sin" would represent a state of psychological anxiety, imbalance, and need. In fact, both grace and sin refer to states of the "soul," one of the words of the lexical field that Jaynes says emerges from preconscious hypostatses.[18] But with the emergence of the authorized self, a grammatical field emerges in which a somewhat structured set of qualitative transformations within the lexical field becomes possible, and this grammatical field enlarges over time as finer distinctions are made about the state, the activity, and the ultimate nature of the original "lexically based" self.[19] However, these transformations still depend on divine referents for their meaning.

The emergence of the empowered self—and especially the work of Kant and those, like Freud, who followed in his footsteps—represents another step increase in the field that allows the mind-space to exist, one we might call a shift from a grammatical field to a "syntactic" field.[20] Kant's approach can be said to be syntactic in two ways. First, his analysis is *self-predicating:* he builds his entire system on the principle of a self-referred description of the subject, in contrast to the grammatical Christian approach, wherein transformations take their importance from the proximity to or distance from God that they express or imply. Kant's analysis is fully centered on the subjective consciousness, both in passive (noumenal) and active (phenomenal) states.

Second, Kant's system begins to establish a matrix of *relationships* that exist between various features of subjective consciousness, not on the basis of the simple, evaluative ("good" and "evil") norms that exist in the grammatical field of Christianity, but with an attempt to allow for the dynamics of tension, interaction, and reinforcement that exist between the various features of subjective human consciousness.[21] Thus, what Kant himself called his attempt at "architectonics" not only identifies "quantity," "quality," "relations," and "modality" in what we perceive but offers a gradient scale to be used with each category.

Quantity	Quality	Relation	Modality
Unity	Positive	Substance-Accident	Possibility-Impossibility
Plurality	Negative	Cause-Effect	Actuality-Nonactuality
Totality	Limited	Reciprocity or Community	Necessity-Contingency[22]

While, in comparison with modern psychological terminology, Kant's categories may seem primitive, schematic, and mechanical, there can be no doubt that Kant opens the door to a far more vast and more complex conceptualization of the features of subjective consciousness than was previously possible.[23] Definition, specificity, and precision increase immeasurably, as does the possibility of subordination of one feature to another without recourse to a priori facts or deistically authorized truth. Quite simply, Kant establishes the foundation upon which a new "field" can be built, one that makes qualitatively different kinds of subjective consciousness possible even as it describes them; he provides a first look inside the labyrinth, which galvanizes the attention of those who follow him.

Perhaps as important is the fact that Kant provides a systematic approach to the analysis of the mind-space of the empowered self. Clearly, it is an "empowered" analysis—that is, self-predicated and hearkening back to no authorizing deity. But, since that empowerment becomes, along with the resonance with the natural world implied by Kant, the feature of his analysis most immediately taken up by his successors, the Romantics, we will postpone a discussion of the significance of Kant's systematic approach. For the Romantics would prove long on sentiment and short on system, and their individualistic innovations would prove limited and, eventually, barren. In the face of that barrenness, systematic analysis will become one of the few tools available to the modern era.

Romantic Individualism

The word "romantic" can conjure up as many conflicting associations as the word "individualism."[24] As Crane Brinton puts it, " 'Romanticism' and 'romantic' are protean words, the despair of a rigorous semanticist."[25] But even Brinton admits that the word "Romantic" applies to a generally accepted body of literature and philosophy, art and music, which shares certain characteristic attitudes about "the true, the good [and] the beautiful"; we need not come up with a rigorous definition of Romanticism to be able to agree with Lilian Furst when she says of one of these characteristics, "It was the real innovation of the Romantics to turn individualism into a whole *Weltanschauung,* to systematize it— in so far as their irrationalism permitted any logical ordering of ideas into a cohesive philosophy."[26] It can be fairly argued that Romanticism represents the first convergence of individualistic attitudes into a social, literary, and philosophical movement that places an emphasis on the solitary individual as nothing less than the center of the universe—at least the universe as seen from the human perspective. As Schlegel says, "It is just his individuality that is the primary and eternal element in man. To make a cult of the formation and development of this individuality would be a kind of divine egotism."[27]

But there is considerably more to Romanticism's individualistic attitudes than an emphasis on self-development, for much of the Romantic movement emerges from the contrast between its own attitudes toward the self and the cosmos and those that had immediately preceded them. It is a commonplace worth repeating that the Romantics saw the eighteenth century as having overrationalized the universe at the expense of the individual's personal and emotional side[28] and that they strove to redress that imbalance by reinstating the emotive and spiritual dimensions of the self to their rightful place. Perhaps it is the image of the Romantic rebel resisting the leveling mechanism of the eighteenth century with an almost godlike conviction that most commonly comes to mind when we think of Romantic individualism: the idiosyncratic genius of Blake, the violent nonconformity of Byron, the defiance of Delacroix's goddess at the barricades, the triumph of Beethoven's symphonic ode. In their passionate, rebellious intensity, the Romantics became a demonstration of the newly awakened power of the individual; they proclaimed, or so they thought, the dawn of a new age of the individual. Yet at the same time as they reveled in the centrality of the self, they began to reveal elements of dissatisfaction with pure individualism that made them simultaneously the apotheosis of individualism and its Indian summer.

As a literary and philosophical movement, Romanticism represents what one might call a celebration of the empowered self. The individual—fully conscious and anxious to test his or her powers of awareness to the utmost—is the overriding Romantic motif, and the attitudes expressed by the Romantic artist are those of the empowered self: the self as the source of truth (in the case of the Romantics, truth as revealed through beauty) and the repository of spiritual meaning; the search for the self as the only avenue to true fulfillment; and—tellingly—the alienation of the self-aware individual, especially the artist, from the mass of humanity.

Perhaps the aspect of Romanticism that most clearly and fully resonates with the individualistic heritage that preceded it is the emphasis on the powers of the individual in the formation of the self. Lukes refers to "the notion of *self-development* [which is] typically Romantic in origin,"[29] but Romantic attitudes toward the individual's power to cultivate personal growth go far beyond the liberal notion of self-development. For the Romantics saw the individual as virtually self-originated; self-discovery amounted to a process of self-creation. Thus the emphasis in Romantic poetry on spiritual autobiography, the record of the solitary individual seeking, finding, and thereby creating a self that is not merely a self-creation but a touchstone for truth, capable of replicating itself. As Wordsworth says of those minds that have achieved self-awareness,

> . . . that glorious faculty
> That higher minds bear with them as their own.
> This is the very spirit in which they deal
> With the whole compass of the Universe:
> They from their native selves can send abroad
> Kindred mutations; for themselves create
> A like existence. . . .
>
> . . . the highest bliss
> That flesh can know is theirs—the consciousness
> Of Whom they are, habitually infused
> Through every image and through every thought.[30]

M. H. Abrams has noted the resonance between the Romantic auto-biography and Augustine's *Confessions,* and he remarks that the Romantic *Bildungsgeschichte* "translates the painful process of Christian conversion and redemption into a painful process of self-formation, crisis, and self-recognition, which culminates in a stage of self-coherence, self-awareness, and assured power that is its own reward."[31] The paramount distinction between *The Confessions* and *The Prelude* is that the latter contains no deistic figure who sanctions the act of self-creation. The self is no longer, as it was with Augustine, "authorized"; the self is *author.* So far does this self-empowerment go that, for the Romantics, the self is the source of meaning not only for itself, but for the things that it perceives around it. As Wordsworth puts it, "Throughout, objects . . . derive their influence not from what they are actually in themselves, but from such as are bestowed upon them by the minds of those who are conversant with or affected by those objects."[32] In effect, the Romantic self is not only author of itself, its powers of perception make it the virtual author of the universe.

This level of empowerment of the self is clearly an extension of—some might say, merely an improvisation on—Kant. Unshaken by the challenge a Hume might make to the validity of "mere" perception, the Romantics not only establish perception as a valid foundation for human reality, as did Kant with his "autonomous will," they install what Kant would call the categorical imperative—the intuitive knowledge of truth—as the principle upon which the glorification of the self could take place. Not only epistemology but beauty itself, once thought an emanation from the radiance of God through the vehicle of nature, became rooted in the individual. This ability to perceive—actually to endow objects with beauty, the highest form of truth—became the basis for the self's commanding stature in the Romantic worldview and the justification for the attention paid to it by philosophers and poets alike. Says Tieck, "Not these plants, not these mountains, do I wish to copy, but my spirit, my mood, which governs me at just this moment.[33] This is the apotheosis of the Kantian worldview: not only does the self find itself the center of experience, it finds the world around it important only insofar as it provides a vehicle for self-expression.

The Romantics were not as thoroughly secular as the rhetoric of their pronouncements on self and truth might lead us to think. Just as the categorical imperative posited a link between the individual and the universe, some Romantics acknowledged just such a link, and their emphasis on the respiritualization of the dry, academic view of life they inherited from the Enlightenment allowed that link to take on religious or at least highly spiritualistic overtones. The self was, in Shelley's famous simile, an Aeolian lyre across which the breezes of experience blow, creating melodies to which the individual sets up harmonic chords. In one sense, this attitude spared the Romantic self the intense isolation that absolute empowerment must inevitably bring about. Mysterious, elusive, and impenetrable, the harmonic resonances between the individual and nature nonetheless afforded the solitary self an accompaniment, a connection of some kind that mitigated the disappearance of theistic underpinnings to human experience.

But this resonance between the individual and nature was itself ultimately an influence in deepening the isolation of the Romantic self. The ability to achieve this resonance came to be seen as a kind of unique talent—or perhaps a universal talent that was uniquely, but only occasionally, realized—that distinguished those who cultivated it, but that also isolated them from their fellows.

> I felt that the array
> Of act and circumstance, and visible form,
> Is mainly to the pleasure of the mind
> What passion makes them; that meanwhile the forms
> Of Nature have a passion in themselves,
> That intermingles with those works of man
> To which she summons him.

So says Wordsworth, calling himself "a renovated spirit singled out . . . for holy services";

> . . . to the open fields I told
> A prophecy: poetic numbers came
> Spontaneously to clothe [me] in priestly robe.

However, Wordsworth does not see himself as a priest ministering to a spiritually eager and devoted humankind. His work is done,

> . . . though (too weak to treat the ways of truth)
> This age fall back to old idolatry,
> Though men return to servitude as fast
> As the tide ebbs, to ignominy and shame.[34]

Though gifted, the Romantic artist "must be lonely, haunted, victimised, devoted to suffering." And Hazlitt's description of the Romantic artist suggests the pass to which the Romantic self was eventually to come: "He is a limb torn from society. . . . The faces of men pass before him as in a speculum; but he is attached to them by no common tie of sympathy or suffering. He is thrown back into himself and his own thoughts."[35] Hazlitt's remarks predate Sartre by a century. However, they might well describe the hero of Sartre's *Nausea,* Camus's *Stranger,* Hesse's *Steppenwolf,* or any one of a number of modern "antiheroes," and they bring us to a pivotal moment in the genealogy of individualism: the moment at which the self, fully empowered and author of itself and the world around it, finds itself utterly isolated, utterly lacking in a substantive connection with anything beyond itself. Characterizing attitudes that had wide currency in the time of Wordsworth and Coleridge but that tell us as much about what was to come in the wake of the Romantic movement, Abrams points out Romantic concepts "which have evolved into the reigning diagnosis of our own age: the claim that man, who was once well, is now ill, and that at the core of the modern malaise lies his fragmentation, dissociation, estrangement, or (in the most highly charged of these parallel terms) 'alienation.' "[36]

"Alienation" is so often used in contemporary discourse that one might take it, as many have, to be a hallmark of the modern and so-called postmodern experiences. The range of topics and disciplines opened up by its use is all but inexhaustible, as has been the commentary on its prevalence in contemporary society. For our purposes, it will be sufficient to examine the relationship between individualism and alienation, particularly the way in which the movement from analog-I to authorized and then to empowered self gives rise to the alienated modern self.

For a paradox lies at the heart of the relationship between the empowered self and the alienated self, and it is a paradox of both outward appearances and inner substance. Outwardly, one must wonder why the apparently triumphant assumption of complete autonomy experienced by the self in the age of individualism—a triumph, as we have seen, that touches the physical, the psychological, and the lyrical spheres of the human experience—should give way so suddenly and so precipitously to the gloomy landscapes of modern attitudes such as existentialism. How, in the short space of twenty-five years, does Beethoven's Ninth Symphony give way to Kierkegaard's *Fear and Trembling?* More substantively, one must ask why the complete self-actualization accomplished by the individual over such an extended time and at such great cost produces such deep feelings of uncertainty and angst; why, after centuries of apparent maturation, does the individual become a stranger in a strange land?

Definitive answers to such questions may be beyond our reach, but an understanding of the relationship that exists between such disparate pairs as the empowered and alienated self, especially the extent to which that relationship is causal, may tell us a great deal, not only about the self in our own time, but about the way in which it will develop in the future. The remaining chapters of this book attempt to examine that relationship and some of the consequences that may spring from it.

7

From Individualism to Authenticity

Authenticity and Alienation

Tracing the relationship between Romanticism and modern alienation, like tracing the threads of individualism itself, can seem a task complicated by an overwhelming degree of complexity. We have the fact that the Romantics themselves exhibited symptoms of alienation similar to, if not the same as, the alienation we associate with the modern experience.[1] We have remarks by Wylie Sypher,[2] suggesting that the liberal tradition has acted as a transmission device whereby the attitudes of Romanticism were carried along into the modern world. But these fragments provide us with a picture no less incomplete than that provided by the many remarks made about the origins of individualism, remarks that offer us the trace of an explanation but do little to expose the deeper structure of the process by which we have inherited the attitudes we now hold. What we need is, again, a genealogical explanation that will provide an understanding of the linkages that exist between Romanticism and modern alienation. Fortunately, an attempt to develop such an explanation exists, and though it displays a number of shortcomings, it helps us see more clearly into the complexities we face.

In his *Sincerity and Authenticity,* Lionel Trilling examines shifts he believes took place after the Renaissance in the way the individual judged the moral content of his or her avowals of feeling—more specifically, in the degree of "congruence between avowal and actual feeling," shifts that Trilling feels begin with the breakdown of social class as a means of measuring individual worth and that lead ultimately to the modern preoccupation with what he calls authenticity.[3]

Trilling argues that a preoccupation with what he calls sincerity originated in the sixteenth century, when a higher degree of social mobility allowed some individuals to leave the social class into which they had been born, even though society as a whole was not yet prepared to acknowledge them as having the requisite "qualities" to enter a new class. Such individuals were suspect because they were like the dramatic villain, "a person who seeks to rise above the station to which he was born."[4] The fact that social mobility thus allowed individuals to appear to be what they were not required a new basis upon which the quality of an individual's character could be assessed. Since it was the shaking—the virtual revolutionizing—of the social fabric that had provoked the need for a new criterion of character assessment, that criterion had to satisfy society's demand to know the worth of an individual, and at the same time it had to be flexible enough to reveal the nature of any individual, regardless of his or her level of social origin. The basis upon which this test of personal character could be made was, ultimately, personal "sincerity"—the degree of congruence between avowal and actual feeling.

Trilling insists that, while we may think of sincerity as an inherently personal criterion, it originated as a social criterion: sincerity was the standard by which one was judged in the eyes of others; it was a means to gaining their trust and confidence rather than a condition sought after as a morally satisfying end in itself. Moreover, societies were expected to be as rigorously sincere as individuals and were judged on the basis of the degree of sincerity they produced among their members. As Trilling puts it, "The intense concern with sincerity which came to characterize certain European national cultures at the beginning of the modern epoch would seem to have developed in connection with a great public event, the extreme revision of traditional modes of communal organization which gave rise to the entity that now figures in men's minds under the name of society."[5] However, this close association between sincerity and society—itself probably a holdover from the Renaissance belief that a congruence between avowal and actual feeling prevented one from falling into the pitfall of deceiving others—was not an enduring one. Ultimately, sincerity became transformed into an end rather than a means, the object of an exclusively personal quest rather than a criterion for determining the value of the individual in society. In the process, sincerity became known by another name, "authenticity," and this transformation took place in no small part as a result of the Romantic reevaluation of the individual's relationship to society.

Trilling cites Rousseau as just one example of the newly emergent attitude toward society and the reassessment of the individual's relation to society. For Rousseau, Trilling says, "the very principle of society . . . is the individual's abnegation of personal autonomy in order to win the forbearance and esteem of others,"[6] and for Rousseau—individualist that he was—such a principle was absolutely unacceptable. The individual must come first; society could never be more than a necessary evil and was nearly always an impediment to individual growth. The "noble savage" was the embodiment of the personal will and strength required to resist the demands of society and preserve the autonomy of the individual; the "sociable" man or woman was the embodiment of the duplicity and hollowness imposed on anyone who would live for the opinion of others.

With Wordsworth and the Romantics, Trilling says, the dissatisfaction with the standards for personal behavior imposed by society fuses with the lingering certainty that some criterion for moral behavior must exist—though at a personal, not a social level—and there emerges the new standard by which one measures the congruence of avowal and actual feeling: authenticity. Taking Wordsworth's "Michael" as the archetypal example of this new standard, Trilling says, "There is no within and without: he and his grief are one. We may not, then, speak of sincerity. But our sense of Michael's being . . . [is] exceptional in its actuality. . . . Michael is as actual, as hard, dense, weighty, perdurable as any stone he lifts up or lets lie."[7] Here, Trilling says, is the essence of the transformation sincerity undergoes as discontent with social determination of personal worth emerges: the character of the individual is measured, not by the extent to which he or she *expresses* a congruence between avowed and actual feeling as a social convention, but by the extent to which the individual *experiences* that congruence, regardless of society's perceptions or interpretations. Where sincerity was a means, authenticity is an end, and one that can be validated only by the individual; those standing outside may encounter, acknowledge, and even experience the authenticity of the individual, but they cannot validate it, for that is only possible for the individual himself or herself.

This attitude suggests the connection that exists between the transformation of sincerity into authenticity and the eventual experience of social alienation that pervades the modern era. Though the balance of his discussion is couched in other terms, Trilling's recounting of the search for authenticity, particularly artistic authenticity, from the Romantic period to the present takes place against the backdrop of a progressive increase in the role of society—perhaps the *presence* of society puts it more aptly—in the life of the individual.[8] The force that Rousseau found so threatening to individual autonomy increases its influence over the lives of all during the nineteenth and twentieth centuries, creating a predictable, yet confounding, situation: the moral individual—one who persists in the search for and the experience of authenticity—becomes progressively more alienated from the social order that not only surrounds him or her but that seems to be gaining in influence and momentum. In fact, if all of us yearn for authenticity, as the Romantics suggest, however unwilling they may be to search for genuine satisfaction for that yearning, then by extension everyone in society experiences alienation from that society; and the greater the degree to which they pursue their desire for authenticity, the greater the degree to which they become alienated.

Thus it is that individualism, by way of the search for authenticity, comes to alienation. "Authentic" comes from the Latin "authenticus," which means "one who does anything with his own hand,"[9] and clearly the fully actualized individual—what we have called the empowered self—is he or she who does *everything* worth doing with his or her own hand. Trilling's "authentic" self represents individualism at its apogee: morally self-authorized and self-validated. However, society is not—indeed, cannot be—comfortable with the "authentic" self, for if the self is the sole authorizing and validating agent, society can have no basis upon which to assess the moral fiber of the individual. By definition, society is a collective, and its assessments must be based on more than one perspective; but by the same token, authentic individualism must spring from the individual's own hand, and as such it remains immune to the validation or condemnation of the collective.

This inherent conflict between pure individualism and society forces us to reconsider the assumptions made above that what we have called "the age of individualism" represented the shedding of external, "authorizing" influences in the individual's determination of truth. For it is clear that individualism, pushed to its limits, is incompatible with the needs of the collective to have some mutual basis upon which to evaluate the worth of the individual, and it must be said that, while the age of individualism represented a profound and revolutionizing shift away from using social criteria upon which to make judgments about personal worth, society still provided the context in which the new, more individualistic attitudes could be realized. Individualists could remain individual and still commit themselves, if not to the maintenance of the status quo (though even this was possible), to the transformation of society.

But once authenticity becomes the preoccupation of what Trilling calls the process of moral revision that takes place in the nineteenth century,[10] society becomes anathema. Rousseau's antagonism becomes Nietzsche's hostility; Hobbes's "that which is not contrary to right reason . . . men account to be done justly"[11] becomes Kurtz's view in *Heart of Darkness* that, as Trilling puts it, "civilization is . . . so inauthentic that personal integrity can be wrested from it only by the inversion of all its avowed principles."[12] The process of shifting from an emphasis on sincerity to an emphasis on authenticity is the final triumph of the individualistic heritage, and the beginning of modern alienation.

Authenticity and Self-Referredness

Another respect in which Trilling's discussion of the post-Romantic era concerns us is in his discussion of the circular nature of the process by which modern art validates itself. Though his discussion is not as succinct as one might hope, in essence it argues that as the influence of society and the consequent alienation of the individual increases, the artistic search for material that is evocative of authentic experience becomes increasingly dependent on evocations of the inauthenticity of modern life. In other words, if the life of the modern individual is becoming increasingly inauthentic, then the only authentic—that is, true to life—artistic statement is the portrayal of inauthenticity.[13] The artist becomes a kind of priest, providing the audience with the experience of the authentic and decrying inauthenticity wherever it may appear.

In Trilling's eyes, the danger implied in this tendency is profound, and though we might not agree with all the implications he divines, the essence of his analysis is pivotal to our own.[14] Trilling argues that, because "the work of art . . . [is] understood to exist wholly by the laws of its own being,"[15] it thus becomes an unreferred and unreferrable entity doomed to perpetual involution: because the inauthenticity of modern life demands "authentic" expression, art, perhaps involuntarily, perpetuates the very inauthenticity it purports to expose, creating an entropic cycle that does little more than intensify with each gyre the degree of inauthenticity that is "authentically" portrayed.

A discussion of modern aesthetics is itself a labyrinth into which our analysis cannot possibly hope to detour, but the underlying concerns of Trilling's discussion speak to questions we ourselves must ask about the nature of individualism in the modern world. For clearly, the implications of the logic that underlies the development of individualism that we have traced are similar to those Trilling assigns to what he calls authenticity. If individualism is, as we have said, the belief system that makes the individual the final arbiter of truth, no matter how admirable the premises that gave that system birth—premises amply demonstrated and held in esteem by the likes of David Riesman[16]—we must ask ourselves what safeguards exist whereby individual self-referredness is protected against the pitfalls in what was originally seen as its source of innovative and liberating strength: the value of subjective personal perceptions. Furthermore, unless we are willing to resign ourselves to the futility of social change, as Trilling seems to do in the closing chapter of his book, we must ask ourselves the consequences of perpetuating individualism when it appears to ensure, if not the collision of opposing forces—society and the individual—then the gradual retreat of one into hermetic solitude as the other accelerates the growth of its influence over the hermetic, insular mass.

These are, as have others in this discussion been, far-reaching questions for which there can be no simple answers. However, if they are viewed within the context of the emergence and eventual triumph of individualistic attitudes, they may offer some insight into the ways in which the dilemmas and paradoxes enfolded within such questions are to be dealt with. Toward that end it may be helpful to recount in a more explicit fashion some of the ways in which Trilling's discussion of sincerity and authenticity dovetails with the development of individualism as we have traced it.

To begin with, there is a clear parallel between the emergence of what we have called possessive individualism and the need, in Trilling's view, for a new criterion—sincerity—for allowing the members of society to judge the personal worth of each individual. What Trilling's discussion does not do, however, is underscore the way in which this development, because it represented a move away from social norms toward more individualistic standards, was a moment of triumph for the individual and a blow dealt to the influence of previous social forms. While Trilling is probably correct in saying that, as a standard for measuring personal worth, sincerity was a criterion that was dominated by social considerations, he does not sufficiently recognize the extent to which this development, since it tolled the end of the more rigid and predetermined standards, such as blood lines, upon which previous social orders were built, was in itself the first step in the alienating process that he ascribes to the post-Romantic period. In other words, one can trace the beginnings of the bitter fruit of social alienation almost to the very moment at which the seeds of individualism began to flower. Once the individual takes it for granted that he or she can determine his or her own worth—a consequence, as we have seen, of the Reformation—then the conflict with society is both immanent and imminent.

Trilling's analysis does not have a great deal to offer us where what we have called subjective individualism is concerned. While he refers to Gusdorf's notion of "internal space" and Lacan's contention that "the development of the '*Je*' was advanced by the manufacture of mirrors," he remains inconclusive about how these developments fit into his analysis. And though he talks of agreement among historians that "in the late sixteenth and early seventeenth centuries, something like a mutation in human nature took place," the importance Trilling ascribes to these psychological changes is that "the idea of society, much as we now conceive it, had come into being." Trilling does suggest ways in which the unconscious becomes a touchstone for the individual in the modern world, largely through the broad acceptance of the unconscious as an "authentic" aspect of human experience, but he does so primarily with the aim of examining what he perceives as the seemingly insoluble conflict between the human unconscious and the demands of the social order in which the individual exists.[17]

Trilling's primary emphasis is upon the way in which the emergence of "authentic man" has come about as a rejection of social demands placed on the individual. But perhaps his failure to isolate fully and identify the inherent reciprocity in this development exposes, not only a shortcoming of his analysis, but a more pervasive modern inability to examine the nature of the conflict between the individual and society—specifically, the way or ways in which that conflict is a dialectic, an almost symbiotic process whereby the growth of one gives rise to a greater degree of alienation from the other, society or individual.

These are matters to which we return in a later chapter. Nevertheless, if both possessive individualism and subjective individualism emerge in conflict with the constraints placed on the individual by society, this is increasingly so with romantic individualism—the source of Trilling's modern "authenticity." Hazlitt's image of the Romantic artist as "a limb torn from society" is, as we have said, one of the most important features of romantic individualism; for Trilling, it is *the* most important feature in the emergence of authenticity as a measure of personal worth. But whatever priority one may give to this feature of the Romantic vision over others, this is clearly the source of the subsequent alienation felt by Romanticism's heirs.

Furthermore, what the Romantic vision fails to transmit to the modern era also helps to account for the bleakness and gloom that characterizes modern alienation. For the Romantics were not, as we have noted in chapter 5, as secular as their pronouncements on the self might lead us to think. Their subscription to belief in the mystically regenerative powers of nature, what Abrams calls "natural supernaturalism," afforded them a cushion against what Camus would characterize as the absurd—the experience of the intensity with which "nature . . . can negate us."[18] But especially with the onset of the industrial era, the technological revolution, and the birth of mass society in the nineteenth and twentieth centuries, the vision of a benevolent natural order begins to evaporate, leaving the individual thoroughly alienated from the social order, but without the redemption afforded by such things as the categorical imperative or the spiritualizing effect of nature. In the absence of a regenerating feature to its outlook, the modern worldview becomes one of "fear and trembling" and "nausea"; the seemingly triumphant, empowered self is reduced to an "irrational man" searching, generally in vain, for merely "the courage to be."

Thus the self, empowered by the triumph of individualistic attitudes that come to flower in the eighteenth and nineteenth centuries, becomes the "authentic," yet alienated, self of the late nineteenth and twentieth centuries. While the emergence of the empowered self brought with it a gradual shedding of what we have called the authorizing elements of the religious and social orders in which that emergence took place, the process of shedding those authorizing elements had not been fully completed when individualism began to flower. The age of individualism, while infinitely more secular than the epochs that had preceded it, maintained a sufficiently supernatural element to soften the harshness of an unmediated confrontation with a universe indifferent to human happiness. These elements do finally evaporate when the Romantic era passes, and they leave the individual standing alone on a bleak cosmological landscape.

Moreover, as the process of secularization finally came to completion, it did so against a backdrop of severe—one might almost say complete—alienation of the individual from the only tangible environment left: society. In the absence of supernatural points of reference such as those available to Kant and the Romantics, the only point of reference that presented itself was society; but society remained inherently unacceptable as a point of reference, not only for purposes of authorization, but even as a means of testing one's own individualistic perceptions. The fully empowered self came to be a fully isolated self, free of the external, "authorizing" influences that had mitigated its empowerment but seemingly immobilized in the void created by their absence.

This brings us back to the question of self-referredness. Trilling raises the issue as an aesthetic one, suggesting that the pervasive inauthenticity of modern life has trapped the artist into believing that only the portrayal of inauthenticity can be considered authentic artistic expression; but we can couch the question in larger terms. How, we must ask, can the empowered, yet alienated, self find an avenue out of its agonizing isolation, if, as a fully self-referred entity, its only point of departure is its own isolation, and its individualistic premises make it— the individual—the only arbiter of truth? Is there anything within the premises of individualism that suggests that the alienated isolation experienced by the individual is subject to question?

The answer is, probably not. Taken to the extreme, individualism is a closed system. It posits the absolute validity of individual assessments of truth, but in so doing—and partly as a function of the fact that it once represented a revolutionary view in conflict with older contending views—it excludes other criteria. The strength of individualism lay in the fact that it liberated the individual from the shackles of superstition and stifling tradition; its weakness lies in the fact that it encloses the individual in a belief system capable only of replicating and validating its own subjectivity.[19] While such a weakness may present no particular problem in an era of good feeling, optimism, and strong social cohesion, such as the Renaissance, it lends itself to the perpetuation of profound despair in darker, more confused times such as we experience in the twentieth century.

Trilling's observation on the plight of the modern artist can be aptly broadened to apply to modern life generally. If isolation and despair are the experience of the modern individual, the question of whether or not that experience is valid is easily answered: because the individual experiences it, it must be so. And because our notions of the validity of human perceptions and their moral "rightness" have historically been so deeply dependent upon one another,[20] we are sometimes led to affirm that alienation and isolation are "right"—or at the very least honest, "authentic," the essence of the human experience.[21]

One of the heirs of the premises of subjective individualism, psychoanalysis, reveals this process at work. Taken as a whole, psychoanalysis can be seen as the ultimate product of the analog-I, the empowered form of the Christian cosmology, the logical extension of Kantian "architectonics." Here is the analog-I under the microscope, scrutinized with the painstaking eye of the trained scientist, mapped and plotted almost as though it occupied physical space. Moreover, as Trilling and others have pointed out, psychoanalysis contains an implied morality, a sense that certain things "should" be, while others should not.[22] However, that implied morality is not dominated by external references; though psychoanalysis is criticized for being normative,[23] its norms are based on an eminent self-referentiality, not on appeals to Deity, property, or a redemptive natural order. The needs of the self are at the center of psychoanalysis.

Freud himself, wrongly characterized in his own time as a perpetrator of "loose" morals, was profoundly aware of the dangers represented by absolute subjectivity and saw psychoanalysis as a force for mitigating those dangers; he might even be termed anti-individualistic.[24] Yet the underpinnings of psychoanalysis remained deeply rooted within the individualistic tradition, as Freud's definitive last work, *Civilization and Its Discontents,* demonstrates. Therein Freud makes the classic statement of the conflict between the individual and society, the conflict between the raging desires of the individual id and the prohibitions placed on satisfying those desires by society. While Freud himself is at least somewhat reflective of the anti-individualistic tradition discussed in the next chapter, his characterization of the conflict between self and society is tellingly individualistic.

Freud sees no resolution to the conflict. He makes a tacit assumption that individual drives are, if not "good," valid features of the human experience, unquestionable facts on the epistemological landscape. Furthermore, Freud resists any suggestion that these drives might be susceptible to transformations that would make them more acceptable to the demands of society; all attempts to do so, he says, merely perpetuate the frustration experienced by the individual, they never lessen it. Again, while he may not endorse their immutability, Freud makes the inevitability of individual drives *and* the improbability of their being significantly and satisfyingly transformed by society both the point of departure and the ultimate conclusion, not only of his last completed book, but of the life's work it represents.

Trilling himself concurs with Freud's view, characterizing it as Miltonic, an acquiescence, with "appalled elation, in the ordeal of man's life in history."[25] But given the overt and implied criticisms of the cult of authenticity that are scattered throughout Trilling's analysis, it seems somewhat surprising that he would be willing to espouse the Freudian view. One must ask, don't the cult of authenticity and psychoanalysis—at least as represented by its characterization of the immutability of individual drives in *Civilization and Its Discontents* and elsewhere—remain entrenched within the self-referred individualistic tradition that establishes the individual perception as irreducible and immutable? Don't both fall into the trap Trilling ascribes to modern artists who take the expression of inauthenticity to be the only authentic artistic endeavor?

Trilling challenges those in the contemporary psychiatric community who would characterize psychosis as a "liberation" from the chains of an inauthentic social reality, asking, "Who that has spoken, or tried to speak, with a psychotic friend . . . will fail to penetrate to the great refusal of human connection . . . express[ed] . . . not to be qualified or restricted by the co-ordinate existence of any fellow man?"[26] Indeed, the very notions of "human connection" and "coordinate existence" seem almost out of place in the cult of authenticity and certainly have no more than problematic significance in the conflict between self and society portrayed in *Civilization and Its Discontents,* where they are seen as practical, not transformational. In neither view does human relationship afford the individual the opportunity to rise above himself or herself. Moreover, the relational side of human existence is all but absent from the lexicon of individualism. While our vocabulary, or "lexical field," is rich in words that describe the epistemology of the individual, it is poor—one might even say nonexistent—in words that describe the epistemology of relationship.

So we are led to two questions. The first is largely prescriptive: has individualism become, in the age of the empowered self, a tautology that draws individuals into deepening isolation where it once liberated them? The second question is largely proscriptive: can the epistemology of relationship provide an escape from the circularity of individualism—and if so, how?

8

Escaping the Labyrinth of the Self

We have seen how the emergence of the self as a key, even preeminent, mode for making assessments of truth developed as individuals became more and more confident about making judgments for themselves, free from the strictures and structures imposed upon them by externals from the state to the church. We have also seen that, as this emergence took place, the "space" occupied by the analog-I increased. One might see this increase as one of size—there being "more" to the analog-I in the time of Kant than in the time of Homer—or simply as an increase in degree of definition in human self-understanding—what was always there was understood with greater precision in Kant's time than in Homer's. But if we are to accept Jaynes's contention that there was a time at which the analog-I, once nonexistent, finally began to emerge, then the increase must be seen in both the domain of size and complexity: the self began to grow and become more complex, while at the same time it began to understand more about itself.

In fact, there is an implied reciprocity between the enhancement of understanding and the size and complexity of the self: an increase in one necessarily implies an increase in the other. As the analog-I learns more about itself, enhancing its powers of understanding, that enhancement enlarges the scope of the analog-I itself, creating nuances and subtleties that had not existed before—and which themselves beckon to be understood, thus perpetuating the process. This self-perpetuating dynamic would appear to be an unexpected blessing bestowed upon human existence by fate, increasing the human capacity for self as that self strove to understand itself, except for one thing: the problem of self-referredness.

We have seen how the gradual withering of connections between the self and society left the self cut off from any point of reference by which it could establish the validity of its perceptions—references that would have by definition been obstacles to the very nature of individualism anyway—and we have encountered Trilling's concerns about how the aesthetic self-referredness of the modern period threatens to become an entropic cycle perpetuating the very inauthenticity it purports to expose. And it seems fair to extend that concern to the dilemma faced by the modern individual, especially given the reciprocal dynamic we have seen between the increase in understanding of the self and the increase in size and complexity of the self itself. For if we establish as our basic premise that the individual self must be the arbiter of all truth, then in order to make confident assessments of truth, the self will have to know itself. However, if, by definition, the process of acquiring self-knowledge enlarges and makes more complex the very thing we are trying to come to understand, then with each attempt to understand, we produce new territory to be explored, new domains with which we must be familiarized, new self-knowledge we must gain.

The consequences of this dilemma are two. First of all, since, as individuals, we feel the profound imperative associated with making accurate assessments of truth, we are unlikely to be satisfied that our assessments *are* true until we have the confidence that comes with complete self-knowledge, something that the reciprocity between the self and its understanding makes unattainable. Second, and perhaps most important for our understanding of the pass to which individualism has come in the modern era, our desire for complete understanding of the self runs the risk of becoming unending exploration of a labyrinth that increases in size and complexity with each new passage explored. Nor can we be comforted by the trick of Theseus—to leave signs where we have previously passed—for the exploration of each passage we encounter creates several more that beckon to us.

Moreover, the goal we pursue is not, at least overtly, escape from the labyrinth of self; what we desire is confidence that our assessments are valid, and only a comprehensive understanding of the labyrinth seems to offer that confidence. The appearance of a new passageway is like a siren's song beckoning us with the possibility of the certainty we seek. A whole variety of trends in modern thought can be seen in this light: phenomenology, with its emphasis on the phenomena of individual human experience as a key to understanding human existence; existentialism, its assertion that existence precedes essence an attempt to make human experience, if not fully fathomable, nonetheless the product of individual choice, and by thus contextualizing it, making it therefore reliable;[1] structuralism, in all its variant forms, an approach to knowledge that attempts to dispel the subjectivity of thought by schematizing it in all its constituent elements, thereby creating a Rosetta stone-like guide to the labyrinth.[2] Even, and perhaps especially, modern psychology, and psychoanalysis in particular, in both their cataloging of the aspects of the personality and in some of their more erudite and radical forms, reveal the tendency to expand on the infinite possibilities of the self.[3] Yet none of these seems to provide the sense of certainty that underlies the search. None seems able to establish the nature of the self in a way that would allow the individual to feel fully confident about his or her assessments of truth. Little wonder, then, that the cry of the modern self has been, to paraphrase a remark made in chapter 1, "I think, therefore I am—but since I cannot be certain about what I am, how can I be certain about the validity of what I think?"

Little wonder, either, that the modern age has ushered in an era of creeping doubt about the efficacy of individualism as a foundation for human conduct. These doubts take shape as a climate of opinion that, in varying degrees, suggests that the belief that the individual can or should be the final arbiter of truth is, at best, an expression of the limitations under which the human animal labors, and at worst, a completely erroneous and misconceived notion.

As was suggested above, Freud is probably an indirect exponent of the first attitude. True, most of Freud's work is well within the individualistic tradition, making the individual an irreducible feature of the epistemological landscape and singularly impervious to all but the most surface of transformations. Given this individual immutability, however, Freud himself reveals a range of attitudes that suggest that he had deep misgivings about the creature he had helped to describe. Philip Rieff has called Freud's attitude "moralistic," saying, "Freud carried the scientific suspicion of nature into ethics,"[4] and indeed one is struck by the degree to which Freud and psychoanalysis, for all their pessimism about the mutability of the individual personality, emphasize distance and objectivity as a goal toward which we must all strive. The objectivity of science is key to Freud's attitude and to the method he uses for examining the individual personality. Of course, it is the pessimism inherent in Freud and psychoanalysis which makes the need for objectivity so urgent: the individual is hopelessly limited by subjectivity in Freud's worldview; as a consequence the most one can hope to accomplish is the mitigation of the effects of that subjectivity by a constant vigilance. In certain respects, Freud is "anti-individualistic," but this attitude is, as we said above, a conservative response to the realities presented by an existence that is presumed to be fully and incontrovertibly individualistic.

In *Individualism Old and New,* John Dewey takes something of a middle ground, critiquing individualism but trying at the same time to defend it in a "renewed" form. Speaking largely in terms of what we have called possessive individualism, Dewey argues that what had once been a force for the bold initiation of ideas that would bring about an improvement in the lot of all has now become a philosophy of "private, pecuniary profit" that, by virtue of its vast success, has transformed society into a mass, created a troubling degree of conformity, and left the individual feeling depressed and lost. But the upshot of Dewey's discussion is that the contemporary dilemma is not a product of individualism but a failure of the individual to remain true to individualistic premises, among which Dewey includes the scientific approach to problem solving. Were we less preoccupied with discovering and maintaining a system "that is true as all others were false," we might recognize that the scientific method teaches us "to break up, to inquire definitely and with particularity, to seek solutions in the terms of concrete problems as they arise." In other words, though Dewey recognizes that individualism has come to a critical pass—and though he sometimes ties this problem to social, rather than individual, realities—his conclusion is that we have too narrowly interpreted the limits of individualism and that we must, on an individual basis, reaffirm the tenets of individualism in the broadest and most inclusive sense. In the end, he remarks, "the depression of the individual is the individual's own responsibility."[5]

While both Freud and Dewey represent a recognition of the fact that something is amiss with the way in which individualistic thinking has served humankind—Freud suspicious of our individual subjectivity, Dewey convinced that individualism has been artificially delimited—neither presents a radical reassessment of the epistemology upon which individualism is based. Both accept that the individual consciousness is primary in human experience, and neither questions the notion that reality is constructed around the singularity and irreducibility of the individual self. For such a reassessment, we must turn to the likes of Karl Marx.

It is not hard to imagine the ways in which Marx and his work present themselves as foils to the individualistic heritage of the West. The emphasis on communal versus individualistic solutions to political and economic problems, the contempt for bourgeois attitudes toward self and society, the insistence that, as Marx himself puts it, "the essence of man is no abstraction inherent in each separate individual":[6] each of these reiterates in both tone and substance the extent to which Marx must be said to represent a conscious and distinct reversal of the individualistic tradition that preceded him.[7] However, to understand truly, not only the way in which Marx represents a reversal of the trend of individualistic thinking, but how that reversal may be a response to the larger problem of the validity of individual assessment of truth, we must go beyond the critique of individualism that Marxist thinking about contemporary social and economic relations implies and uncover the basis upon which it is built—a basis that lies in a radical rethinking of individualistic premises.

It is worth noting that Marx began his career with a close study of Hegel, whom he eventually criticized for having a Romantic philosophical attitude that "descends from heaven to earth." In one sense, Marx's rejection of Hegel is both a rejection of one important aspect of the Romantic legacy and also the pivot upon which his reversal of the individualistic heritage takes place. For, as we saw in chapter 5, the Romantics responded to the increasing alienation of the individual from the social environment with a leap into the supernatural, a belief that individuality itself somehow partook of the divine. In Hegel, that leap took the form of an assertion that History was the will of God acting itself out in the lives of humankind and that all analysis must follow from this premise. Marx leapt upon that premise and insisted that it must be turned on its head: that all analysis must base itself upon, as he puts it, "real, active men, and . . . their real life process."[8] In other words, Marx essentially takes the final secularizing step that the Romantics could not, rejecting any possibility that forces beyond the direct experience of "real men" might influence their lives, and insisting that any pronouncements about history must be inductive, rather than deductive.[9]

This assumption brings Marx to an important reconsideration of the nature of the individual. By insisting that the discussion begin from the lives of "real men"—the plurality of human existence—Marx sets himself up in opposition to an important feature of Romantic individualism: the belief that the individual self exists independent of, often even in opposition to, other selves. While this insular feature of individualism is rarely explicit, it is implied in each of the individualistic attitudes we have examined, for each presupposes a priori an individual self that exists as a self-conscious entity and that subsequently interacts with its environment. Selfhood *and* self-awareness, it might be said, precede engagement with the rest of the world; furthermore, since both selfhood and self-awareness have such a high premium placed on them within the individualistic system of beliefs, both are seen as having inviolability, whether in relation to other individuals (as in possessive individualism), other realities (as in epistemological individualism), or society (as in romantic individualism). Not only are selfhood and self-awareness inherent, they are not to be interfered with.

For Marx, this approach to the individual was a deus ex machina, a deductive principle imposed upon the real world from above. He insisted that the process be reversed, that one must begin with the "real life processes" of individuals and proceed inductively to characterizations of human nature; and he believed that when this was done, the unassailability of selfhood and self-consciousness is exposed as a defensive reaction built on an indefensible premise. For, Marx says, observation of "real men" reveals that consciousness—personal, individual consciousness of the kind represented by Jaynes's analog-I—is not a given, not an "abstraction inherent in each individual": consciousness emerges out of the interaction of individuals with one another, it springs from "the material intercourse of men." Put simply, "Consciousness is . . . from the very beginning a social product."[10]

At first glance, this might seem in direct contradiction to one of the basic tenets of this study, for we have approached our discussion of individualism with the solitary individual in mind. However, it is important to distinguish between the emphases that individualism and its genealogy have perpetuated and the bases upon which an examination of that genealogy is made. Certainly it is fair to say that individualism posits the singular, perhaps one might even say insular, individual as the cornerstone of the system of beliefs it represents. However, the acknowledgment of that singularity or insularity as a valid presupposition has not been inherent in our tracing of individualism's genealogy. In fact, the premise of either singularity or insularity would seem insupportable in the face of the seed from which our genealogy has sprung: the emergence of the analog-I.

For, it will be remembered, Jaynes suggests that the emergence of the analog-I—itself a breakdown of the bicameral mind that had once allowed individuals to be controlled by the "voices" of gods that they had internalized and obeyed—might have taken place as a consequence of "the forced violent intermingling of peoples from different nations, different gods, the observation that strangers, even though looking like oneself, spoke differently, had opposite opinions, and behaved differently."[11] Moreover, Jaynes remarks that it is unlikely to have been coincidence that Assyria, the "key nation in this development" was also the nation that was most engaged in trade with other nations.

In other words, not only is it apparent that Marx's thought is a reversal of the individualistic tradition that we have thus far traced and that his reversal is based on an interpretation of individual consciousness radically different from that which seems to have been inherent in the emergence of individualism, but Marx's conception seems to be more in accordance with the basis upon which we have conducted our investigation than the basis upon which individualism itself is built. That this should be so should not be too surprising. While the emergence of the analog-I must be said to have opened the first of a long series of doors that would lead ultimately to the emergence of the self as a fully empowered entity in the age of individualism, the original analog-I cannot have been expected to recognize—or necessarily even remember[12]—that its emergence took place as a function of an interaction. Having seemed to spring out of its own head, the analog-I assumed itself as a first cause and proceeded along the path we have traced.[13] Only with the advantage of hindsight can we begin to appreciate the difference between the simple emergence of consciousness and the interactive development that consciousness probably was.

A strict Marxian approach might lead us from this point toward more careful scrutiny of the structure of material relations within Assyrian society and between that society and its neighbors. However, our purpose is not to adopt a Marxian approach but to continue with the genealogical analysis Marx's contribution helps to enlighten. For indeed, the notion that consciousness may have been the consequence of an interaction between individuals, rather than the experience of a solitary individual, certainly casts a new light on our discussion, especially where the nature of the relationship between the individual and society is concerned. As we have seen, it was the conflict between self and society that helped give rise to the cult of authenticity and, ultimately, to the painful alienation to which individualism seems to have bestowed upon modern life. Furthermore, that conflict was regarded—by Rousseau, the Romantics, and even Freud—as elemental, the result of the incompatibility of personal integrity (or, alternatively in the Freudian view, individual instincts driving for satisfaction) and the demands of society. So it would seem appropriate to return to that conflict and analyze it with the assumption that society and social relations may not necessarily be antithetical to either the integrity or the satisfaction of the individual.

Here it may be helpful to remind ourselves of Colin Morris's remark quoted above in chapter 1 that "the hard core of . . . individualism lies in the psychological experience . . . of a clear distinction between my being and that of other people." In this characterization we see clearly what we might tend to miss in Jaynes's—the distinct line of demarcation between the being of one individual and that of another. Jaynes's remarks, written about a time in which social bonds were vastly more dominant in the life of the individual—indeed, were only just beginning to give way to the recognition of individuality—place the "difference" in a social context, as they should, which gives them a more neutral cast. Morris's characterization, however, partly because it is a statement of psychological "truth" made outside of any particular historical context, highlights the extent to which the notion of a "clear distinction" becomes a *division* that in and of itself might be said to plant the seed of alienation between self and society that eventually emerges; clearly the development of individualism is in part a consequence of an emphasis on division between individuals, rather than mere contrast among them.

That this should be so is, again, very understandable. Even in Jaynes's historical and anthropological account, in which social context plays a significant role in uniting individuals, it is not hard to imagine "difference" becoming "division." Indeed, the very fact that the awareness of difference may have come, as Jaynes suggests, from the interaction between different societies with different "bicameral voices" leaves open the very strong possibility that the emergently conscious self associated its newly found consciousness with its own society and drew lines of demarcation that distinguished between things that were familiar and things that were not. Alternatively, emergently conscious individuals may have returned from journeys during which their bicameral voices ceased to function and found themselves permanently alienated from their own societies by virtue of the fact that the members of their society still heard and responded to those voices while they did not.[14]

In either case, it seems reasonable to expect that eventually differences would become perceived as divisions between individuals, features that set them apart from one another, and this step would no doubt have eventually led to the emergence of conflict and a sense of opposition among individuals. Moreover, it is not hard to imagine how the emergence of consciousness would have proceeded in a manner that would allow the emphasis on distinction that Morris emphasizes. For though the encounter with others may have helped to provoke consciousness, it would not necessarily provoke in the emergently conscious individual the realization that others might have consciousness as well; consciousness would no doubt have been experienced as a uniquely personal and individual development, at least at first. Furthermore, it would seem only natural that once a sense of individuality emerged, the feature of human experience made possible by consciousness, it would be explored—as we have seen that it was. The domain of consciousness/individuality would continue to expand and grow in complexity, and as it did, the line that existed—or seemed to exist—between the self and everything else, would become that much more distinct, that much more elemental to the human experience.

Therefore it can hardly be surprising that individualism, the belief system that emerged out of the experience of consciousness and individuality, eventually became an ideology of opposition to society. Consciousness itself began, however involuntarily, as a challenge to certain social bonds—namely, those that held together individuals who heard the same bicameral voices. Individualism merely formalized the bases upon which that rejection had occurred and incorporated into its canon the perceptions that had come with newly emergent consciousness, among them "the psychological experience . . . of a clear distinction between my being and that of other people." The impinging of anything from outside the domain of individual being was seen as a negation of that being and therefore unacceptable.

At the outset, the history of the emergent self was, as we have seen, simply an expansion of the domain in which the self felt comfortable claiming as its own: the development of the analog, authorized, and empowered "selves." But since this development involved the increase of individual self-confidence in making choices that had previously been made for the individual by religious, social, and political tradition, there emerged, rightly or wrongly, an implied assumption that, as

Ruth Benedict puts it, "what was subtracted from society was added to the individual." Eventually, this assumption led to the positioning of the individual and society in mutually antagonistic roles: the individual existed within the domain of his or her "distinction," and society threatened to dissolve the lines of distinction and submerge each individual "in an overpowering ocean."[15]

Here again it is easy to understand why society—which had actually been seen as providing support for the individual through the time of the Enlightenment—came to appear in such an antagonistic light. As seen through the eyes of the Romantics, society was neither the "natural" backdrop against which all human life was lived, as was the case in the Renaissance, nor the device by which human relations were rationally ordered, as was the case in the Enlightenment. Society was made threatening to the Romantics by its heartless, despiritualizing character, characteristic of the kind of society sociologists have come to call, after Tonnies, gesellschaft. Ironically, though Benedict is right in arguing that the antagonism between the individual and society is a "misleading misconception" perpetuated by the nineteenth century, it must be said that the disappearance of the gemeinschaft—the more natural and "organic" forms of social organization—was due in part to the adoption of greater and greater responsibility by the individual. Though the effect was unintentional, the empowerment of the self gradually drained tradition of its vitality and left it an entity that was more voluntaristic, structural, and, for the Romantics, spiritually toxic.

Put simply, the gradual assumption of a greater and greater range of prerogatives by the individual narrowed the extent of society's influence over the individual, but it also delimited the extent to which society could provide revitalization for the individual. This latter function of society is a critical one, and Benedict puts it well when she says, "In reality, society and the individual are not antagonists. His culture provides the raw material of which the individual makes his life. If it is meagre, the individual suffers; if it is rich, the individual has the chance to rise to his opportunity."[16] Benedict is perfectly right in challenging the assumption that society's gain is the individual's loss, and vice versa; however, it is possible that intense focus on one of these will result in the atrophy of the other, especially if the nature of that focus is, as it has been throughout what we have called the age of individualism, based on a premise that obstructs the reciprocal process by which individuals invest themselves in the social order.

It was not society that was the culprit, but the drained society that had resulted from the extended emphasis placed on the importance of the individual at the expense of society. While the assumption that the individual and society are necessarily locked in some elemental and irresolvable conflict may be a false one, very much rooted in the Western experience of a mere two centuries, the development of individualism over a much longer period of time has focused attention on the exercise and enhancement of *individual* powers, not social skills, and as a consequence society has seemed to become more and more remote from—even antagonistic to—human development. Actually, it has simply been relegated to a secondary position, and that position has kept it from keeping pace with the remarkable transformation that has taken place in the individual over the course of time.

But if the dichotomy between self and society is a false one and the nature of the consciousness from which individualism has sprung is the product, not simply of the epistemological singularity of the human individual but of the plurality of the human experience, then the uncovering of this false dichotomy may represent an opportunity to provide an avenue out of the dilemma of self-referredness. For if the labyrinth of the self is not the single, elemental unit of the human experience that individualism has allowed us to think it is, then one can argue that the human experience—taken now in its more proper, pluralistic sense—includes an inherently parallactic element in the very plurality that constitutes it.

Modern anthropology provides us with the foundations upon which we can make the argument that *other* selves—even society at large—provide the referredness that Trilling fears is lacking in the modern condition. For anthropologists assume that the human species is, by definition, social; as one commentator puts it: "Human history began at the point where *hominid* progenitors became human, i.e., when they had attained a sufficient development of foresight, communication, and tradition . . . [to allow us to say that] this hominid can no longer survive without the assistance of culture (is dependent on *cultural* means of adaptation), and hence is no longer an animal but has crossed the threshold of humanity."[17]

Perhaps one of the earliest comprehensive attempts to demonstrate the phenomenology of cultural influence on the identity of the individual comes in George Herbert Meàd's *Mind, Self, and Society*. Mead, a pragmatist, proposes a conceptual dyad very close to Jaynes's analog-I as a means of illuminating the dualism implied in a conception of self that allows the individual to be "of two minds";[18] and Mead does so in a fashion that emphasizes the social nature of that conception. Starting from the assumption that symbolic communicative ability is that which distinguishes human nature from other biological forms, Mead takes a microscopic look at the communicative act, arguing that any communicative gesture requires the assumption of a response, or range of possible responses, on the part of the individual to whom the gesture is directed; in other words, that aspect of human nature that distinguishes it from all others—the communicative act—is interactive, requiring both source and audience. The assumption of a response is both an empathetic and imaginative act, Mead says, which requires the communicator to formulate, within himself or herself, a kind of parallel (Jaynes would say "analog") self wherein the attitudes of others are anticipated, harbored, felt, weighed, judged, and so forth. Thus, Mead argues, we come to consist of two selves: the "I," the spontaneous self that reacts to its environment; and the "me," the "organized set of attitudes of others which one himself assumes."[19]

There are many problems with Mead's formulation. He argues, for instance, that the "I" and the "me" cannot exist simultaneously,[20] contradicting a whole body of reflective and self-scrutinizing experience from seventeenth-century metaphysical poetry to modern ego psychology. More seriously, Mead's positivistic and behavioristic approach leads him to a dangerous conformism: "How can we take the individual with his particulars and bring him over into a more nearly uniform type of response?" he asks, in characterizing the goals underlying his and modern psychology's efforts, thus allowing himself to paint a picture of the self that is, at bottom, virtually determined by society through sophisticated mimicry.[21] Moreover, his account fails to explain whether the source of the communicative impulse is social or personal—a critical question in the complicated chicken-and-egg puzzle he tries to assemble.

Nevertheless, Mead's work enlarges the bulk of evidence suggesting that a profound symbiosis exists between the emergence of the individual self and the emergence of society and culture: "the learned behavior patterns, ideas and values acquired by man as a member of a *social* group."[22] Moreover, not only does this evidence seem to reinforce the suggestion that the emergence of Jaynes's analog-I must have been a reciprocal event of some kind, it also belies the assumption that the individual is or must be the elemental, irreducible unit of epistemology.

For if human nature emerges out of a social context, rather than a purely individualistic one, then any assessment of truth must, by definition, be subjected to scrutiny on the basis of pluralistic, rather than merely individualistic, criteria. And therein lies a cutting edge that may be said to cut the Gordian knot of self-referredness.

If the human experience is social as well as solitary, pluralistic as well as individualistic, then it is fair to say that any human enterprise, if it is undertaken in a balanced and truly *human* fashion, comprises both the social and the individual and does not meet the test of truth until it has met criteria that represent both the social and individual features of human experience. This is not to say that all human endeavor is composed equally of both features. Marriage, for instance, may be conceived by many Western societies as a matter of purely individual choice, while the deterioration of the environment may be seen as a matter of largely social concern. However, since the bearing of children in a rapidly overpopulating world may have an adverse effect on the environment, and the deterioration of the environment has implications for each individual, it is naive to imagine that either can be treated in isolation as matters of purely personal or social concern. Nor can one insist that in all cases one must have precedence over the other. The social and the personal exist in *reciprocal* relation to one another: as two interdependent features of the human existence, each has implications for any aspect of human behavior, and a claim for absolute exclusivity or priority for either can only do damage to both.

More specifically, it would seem that the emphasis placed on personal, individual truth by the Western heritage, especially the individualistic tradition of the last two or three centuries, while it has clearly made great contributions to the enrichment of human experience and the enhancement of human self-determination, has suffered from a one-sided emphasis that is both uncharacteristic of the human experience and ultimately incompatible with the conditions from which the first seeds of that individuality emerged. That emphasis was not, for the most part, felt as a disadvantage until modern times because of the vast range of possibilities it opened up to the human individual and the broad spectrum of individual talents and skills that were uncovered and nurtured under its aegis. However, two dimensions of the modern experience began to reveal the shortcomings of the personal, individualistic emphasis: the failure of individualism to produce a referentiality that would prevent it from becoming lost in the labyrinth of personal experience, and the despiritualization of society that led to the setting up of a false dichotomy between self and society. We have sketched the outlines of the first of these, and the second is sufficiently broad to warrant a far more extended discussion than is possible here, but it is worth reiterating the two side by side to make absolutely clear how they seem to portend what we might call the closing of the age of individualism.

Since the very nature of self-awareness—at least as it is perpetuated by the exploratory style of what we have called subjective individualism—generates new "territory" of which the individual must be aware, and since individualism neither requires nor provides for the testing of individual perceptions against criteria set up outside the domain of those perceptions, the process of self-discovery threatens to become a narcissistically self-perpetuating one. In the end, the individual feels no more confident about his or her perceptions than was possible at the outset of the search, and the failure to find grounds for confidence becomes that much more unbearable for the incredible weight of isolation and solitude that the process of self-discovery accrues.

At the same time, since the emergence of consciousness initiated a process whereby the self came to rely more and more on itself and less and less on society for its assessments of truth, the gradual despiritualization of society took place as individuals withdrew their investment in society as a form of spiritual regeneration and placed it more and more with themselves. The natural direction of that process combined with the understandable division of the world by the individual into the self and the not-self to create an implied conflict between society and the self; in the end, not only had society come to be seen as that which had stood between the individual and full empowerment, but its culpability seemed confirmed by the spiritual decline into which it had fallen as it became stripped of the richness and color represented by gemeinschaft and blighted by the sterility of gesellschaft.

But here too, the individual became the ultimate bearer of the burden represented by the despiritualization of society, for the cost of freedom from strictures placed on the individual by society was a profound alienation. At first the individual felt alienated only from society, as was the case with the Romantics. But eventually that sense of alienation linked up with the burden of loneliness imposed on the self by the subjective legacy of its odyssey of self-discovery, so that in the end the self felt alienated, not only from society, but from itself.

These two features of the modern condition, each a seemingly insoluble problem, both spring from false assumptions implicit in the individualistic tradition. Moreover, neither yield to resolution unless one steps outside of the premises upon which they are based: the primacy of individual, subjective perceptions and the inherent conflict between self and society. However, when one assumes that the emergence of consciousness—and therefore of everything upon which individualism is based—springs from an interactive, rather than a solitary, source, then the limitations of the individualistic tradition reveal themselves and we are presented with opportunities for stepping beyond the labyrinth of the self and the antagonistic view of self and society. And in that the resolution to the dilemma of modern individualism requires us to step outside of, even challenge, such basic premises of the individualistic tradition, it seems fair to say that the age of individualism is at a close.

9

Beyond Individualism

It is a truism that, while anthropologists deal with millennia almost casually, intellectual historians do so at their own risk. Yet an analysis such as we have just completed leaves some important questions unanswered, some of which spring from the decidedly anthropological bias this discussion reveals and the consequent necessity of dealing with huge sweeps of time not frequently addressed by intellectual history. For if we are bold enough to suggest that individualism represents a several-millennia-long development that emphasized one side of human experience, individual subjectivity, at the expense of another, pluralistic intersubjectivity, the reader is certainly warranted in asking how, or perhaps even whether, this second aspect can be nurtured and made to grow. To this question, even (and especially) the anthropologically minded intellectual historian must answer prognostically rather than prescriptively.

Intellectual history generally interweaves itself so naturally and so subtly with problems of philosophy, morals, and ethics that it almost inevitably poses responses to questions it set out simply to identify and analyze. Taking this added step need not be a problem if the analysis is a sound one; in fact, the result may be a major contribution to the philosophical issues that are thus engaged. However, we cannot let our desire to answer philosophical questions cloud our ability to recognize what is answerable and what is not, nor can we let our need for certainty allow us to fault a discussion that cannot move quickly from analysis to prescription. The foregoing discussion certainly falls into this category, and it does so precisely because of the vast range of human development that it tries to encompass. Though the urge to immediately prescribe (and proscribe) certain forms of behavior as a means of moving on beyond individualistic premises may be great, the relative poverty of our knowledge about what lies beyond individualism should warn us about the dangers of coming to any quick or summary conclusions.

It is possible to say that we now know a great deal about individualism and its legacy in the West; it is also possible to say that we have found some shortcomings in the premises upon which individualism has been built, and the discovery of those shortcomings helps to untie some of the knottier questions now facing us. So little more do we know than that, however, that even if we assert that we are at the dawning of a new age (and who knows? we may still be in the grip of a dying one), we would be hard put to name it appropriately. The superficiality of popular attempts to do so,[1] however well intentioned they may be, only underscores how vast and complex the emergence of a new age really is, and how ill equipped those who first recognize it are to give any detailed account of it, let alone to prescribe behavior for expediting its emergence.

I would therefore caution those who would see in the closing of the age of individualism a justification for invoking morality or ideology as a means of moving things along. Obviously, one of the most readily available bases for moral and ideological prescriptions built on an analysis such as we have conducted here is the socialist worldview, especially that represented by the work of Marx, and it can hardly be coincidence that socialism emerged as an ideology in the wake of the final phase of individualism.[2] However, we must be careful not to reverse the positions of phenomena and generalizations—or, as Marx himself would put it, we must begin from the "real life processes" of the human species and proceed to extrapolate from them; we cannot afford to begin with extrapolations and prescribe behavior from them.

The advent of socialism is a phenomenon that most definitely reflects a move away from individualistic premises toward communalistic ones and as such is further evidence that such a shift may be underway as the shortcomings of a purely individualistic view become more evident. However, the shift itself is a generalization derived from "real life" evidence and cannot be used simplistically as a justification for invoking socialism, in whatever form, as the "one true path" into the future. Insofar as socialism, or Marxism, reflects a genuine cultivation and nurturing of those aspects of the human experience overlooked by individualism, then they represent reasonable avenues for exploration and discovery in much the same way Christianity once represented such an avenue for uncovering aspects of the singular individual that had not yet been developed. However, any perspective that demonstrates a genuine ability to cultivate and nurture the pluralistic, interactive side of human nature must be considered legitimate ground for exploration, and all such perspectives must be subject to scrutiny and criticism; if we do indeed stand on the threshold of an age in which the interactive side of human nature is to expand and grow, mutual discussion and critical dialogue must, by definition, be the vehicles by which that age is to unfold.

While we must be very careful about using our understanding of the close of the age of individualism to prescribe and proscribe behavior, we do have sufficient understanding of the process whereby individualism itself emerged to speculate, if not on how we *should* usher in a new world view, then on how that world view *might* be expected to emerge and take hold.[3] In other words, rather than using our analysis as a basis for prescription, we may justifiably use it as a basis for developing a prognosis of the ways in which an intersubjective world view may establish itself.

In *The Origins of English Individualism,* Alan Macfarlane makes a remark about those origins that is both tantalizing and frustrating in its incompleteness; admitting that his book has not found the roots of individualism, he says, "I have my own suspicions as to where the 'origins' were in time and space and they are similar to those of Montesquieu: 'it is from [the ancient Germans] the English have borrowed their idea.'"[4] The present discussion has not chosen to touch on the ways in which elements of other cultures, as opposed to interactions between them, may have contributed to the development of individualism, though such contributions no doubt existed and may indeed have included the influence Macfarlane suggests. However, if we take Macfarlane's remark as a suggestion of how the development of such things as individualism are reinforced once the seed has been sown, then we may properly ask ourselves whether or not anything in the contemporary world may represent a parallel influence, this time contributing, not to the development of individualistic tendencies and assumptions, but to an intersubjective, pluralistic world view.

Given that we have traced the emergence of individualism in a context that is largely Western and eventually capitalistic, one might expect that the most productive search for such influences or parallels would take place outside the confines of that world, and indeed an emergent body of literature suggests, both directly and indirectly, that individualism is a largely Western belief system and that other, non-Western traditions contain elements that are in sharp contrast to the individualistic tradition of the West.

One of these works is entitled, appropriately enough, *The Public Man*. Subtitled "An Interpretation of Latin American and Other Catholic Countries," the author, Glen Caudill Dealy, sets out to analyze certain disparities he feels exist in the interpretations of Latin American culture made by those who come from a Western, Protestant background. Dealy's aim is to demonstrate that many forms of behavior that those, especially Americans, who come from a capitalistic tradition regard as wasteful, lazy, unproductive, or random are actually part of a system of norms, goals, and values as tightly structured and clearly directed as those in Western capitalist societies. The problem, Dealy argues, is that Westerners fail to imagine that behavior could be based on any premises other than the highly rationalistic, goal-oriented ones upon which they operate; as a consequence, they miss entirely the very logical—though very different—pattern that accounts for a variety of "perplexing" behavior on the part of Latin Americans, from lateness for appointments to an apparent preference for form over substance.

Today, the analysis of misinterpretations across cultures is almost a commonplace.[5] However, what is important about Dealy's analysis is the center around which he says Latin American—and most Catholic—cultures revolve. Tracing the Latin American heritage back, through the Catholic tradition to Augustine and Aquinas, Dealy argues that the perpetuation of Catholic forms in countries where the Reformation did not have as significant impact as in countries such as Germany and Great Britain (he cites examples from Italy, Spain, Ireland, and Poland) prevented the merging of the public and private self that took place in Reformation theology. Augustine, Dealy says, established a "classical division between the values of the public world and those of religion"; for some time that division remained an insoluble dilemma, dividing the individual's attention between the public and the private life. But Aquinas resolves the problem:

> It was the greatness of Aquinas that he recognized the Augustinian dichotomy for what it was—an existential abyss. In Aquinas's endeavor to inte-

grate Aristotle with Christianity he perceived the need for, and carried forward, the classical secular value structure, a value structure oriented toward *public activity* that was eminently fitted for life in the medieval city. . . .

Thus the new ethic for the Earthly City was Catholic in its modern conception. But its roots were in the classical tradition. Above all, it was a secular ethos. It reflected the consequences of assuring one's salvation through institutionalized intermediaries and the use of indulgences. With the major problem of afterlife resolved, men turned toward their basic drive for self-realization.[6]

Thus, Dealy argues, the failure of the Reformation to take hold in Spain allowed the perpetuation of an Augustinian/Aquinian world-view that was subsequently transplanted to Latin America (and that exists in some form in other contemporary Catholic countries). In that worldview, the powerful force toward self-realization, which one would expect to have been as powerful in Catholic countries as in non-Catholic, found its satisfaction in public, and largely political, activity, rather than in private, economic activity. Diverted from the intense preoccupation with demonstrating their "election," which, as we saw in chapter 5, motivated Protestant thought, the Catholic worldview took a different route.

> Aquinas provided that Catholic man, once delivered from the need for actively working out his own other-worldly destiny, could turn toward the public. Henceforth, a Catholic, unlike a Protestant, need not impress the public with his being of the elect in order to prove to *himself* that he was saved. Rather, he could turn toward the pre-Christian, classical tradition for his ideas of immediate self-gratification and achievement. This was the accepted premise of public action.

In other words, where the Protestant was locked in "introspection, loneliness, and a general realization of worldly asceticism in pursuing [his or her] own salvation through private activity," a process whereby, as we have seen, the empowering of the highly individualized self was given its greatest thrust forward, the Catholic took an alternative path, finding self-satisfaction, not in private, individualistic self-realization, but in public—and, one might argue, therefore decidedly more plural-istic—forms of achievement.[7]

Other analyses of Latin American culture complement Dealy's, one of which we will encounter shortly. However, another analysis of non-

Western traditions deals even more directly with the question of individualism as a uniquely Western phenomenon. *Rugged Individualism Reconsidered* is a collection of essays by anthropologist Francis L. K. Hsu that represent a lifetime of largely ethnographic research devoted to demonstrating that the individualistic hegemony that has dominated contemporary Western scholarly and popular thinking is a false one that fails to account for the great majority of cultures and peoples in the world.

Like Dealy, Hsu argues that the narrow, even chauvinistic, outlook of the West has kept it from seeing that patterns of behavior in other cultures, while they may seem strange and "inscrutable," must be examined from outside the set of assumptions that Western scholarship often brings to them, and that when they are, the observer comes to recognize that much that is apparently random or irrational is really based on a set of clearly related premises that simply differ from those of the West. Moreover, Hsu's book singles out the individualistic heritage of the West for special scrutiny and, ultimately, criticism, arguing that individualism not only represents a limited set of beliefs but that by exercising a hegemonic dominance over the Western world view, it has greatly atrophied very essential features of the human experience for those who fall under its influence.

Rugged Individualism Reconsidered is a virtual laundry list of the ways in which other cultures, largely Asian, exhibit patterns of behavior, goals, and norms that contrast sharply with the individualistic heritage of the West. Perhaps the most powerful and penetrating statement of the importance of the contrast between the two orientations takes place in Hsu's essay "Eros, Affect, and *Pao*." Using a complex matrix for characterizing cultural attributes that he had developed in an earlier essay, Hsu argues that Western societies differ from Eastern in that they place a great deal of emphasis on *eros*—the raw sex urge felt on a personal level—and much less on *affect*—the emotions and attachments that tie one to people, entities, and institutions beyond the individual self. Hsu characterizes this difference as being parallel to that between precious metal and specie, adding, "Until gold (or silver or cowrie shells) is transformed through legal fiction into money, its circulation is limited"; not until value is placed on a given currency can it be used to bind individuals together.[8]

In the West, Hsu argues, the discontinuity between past and present (the absence of dominant traditions) and the emphasis on individual volition produce a society in which satisfaction is highly personal, leading to a high erotic quotient, but to a very diminished level of affect. In the East, Hsu says, the satisfaction of raw sexual urges has less importance than the ties the individual shares with family, friends, and society. "The crude sex urge will remain important on the personal level but it can at best unite a few individuals. . . . When it is transformed into affect, it is then more heavily regulated by law and custom and channelized into common expressions by culture . . . and may eventually even serve as an agent to bind different societies together."[9] So far has the Eastern tradition gone toward transforming individual orientation into a preoccupation with wider familial and social bonds, Hsu says, that the Chinese tradition can actually be characterized as having taken a step beyond specie and having produced the equivalent of a credit instrument: *pao.*

Translated literally, *pao* means "reciprocity." But as a feature of Chinese life, it is far more than a tit-for-tat world view. "The most generalized ingredient underlying even relation-specific virtues such as *hsiao* (filial peity) and *chung* (loyalty)," Hsu says that *pao* informs every aspect of Chinese behavior, not simply with a belief in the importance of repayment of all kinds, but in *an intrinsic value placed on the ability to extend one's generosity in the broadest way possible.* "In the same sense as a departed ancestor shading his descendants like a tree, a living man who can spread his personal shade to cover a large number of clansmen (and others if he is in a position to do so) is a more important man in the kinship group than another man who is unable to do so."[10] Thus *pao* is more than mere aquiescence to the demands of the social contract such as described by Freud in *Civilization and Its Discontents.*[11] *Pao* represents a value placed on the ability to serve as a benefactor to one's fellows; it is, as Hsu says, quoting another analysis of the phenomenon,[12] a fundamental orientation of "response."

Hsu does not see *pao* as a panacea to the ills of the human species. He demonstrates that, while it serves to bind groups together much more enduringly than the more erotic Western orientation, it also has the drawback of creating a more inflexible and unchanging culture and, taken to one extreme, can "become more and more a matter of pure business: exchange without sentiment."[13] In the same way, the erotic, individualistic orientation of Western society can, pushed to the extreme, produce a centrifugal force that atomizes society.

The importance of an orientation such as *pao* for the purposes of our discussion is twofold. First, it represents—as does the "public man" attitude demonstrated by Dealy in Catholic countries—an attitude that exists in stark contrast to the individualistic attitudes that have not only dominated the West for centuries but that have been taken rather chauvinistically to be the primary perspective from which problems of human existence should be cast. Second, the orientation represented by such attitudes as *pao* and the world view of the "public man" not only present us with a contrast to the orientation that individualism has produced in the Western capitalist world, but they also offer an astonishing degree of complementarity to that orientation where the question of breaking out of the circularity of individualism is concerned.

Consider the attitude represented by *pao*. We saw above in chapter 8 that one of the problems facing contemporary Western civilization has been the despiritualization of society, which took place as a consequence of the increased emphasis on individualism that accompanied the empowerment of the self. It might be easy to imagine—as do Freud, Trilling, and others—that the alienation of the individual from society is an inescapable feature of the human condition, that individuals will always be alienated from society. Yet this assumption is tenable only from a rather myopic, exclusively Western (and, those in the Marxian camp would add, capitalistic) point of view. For Hsu's work, along with Dealy's and that of others,[14] makes clear not only that isolated individuals can experience a high degree of integration into society but that entire cultures can be based on an orientation as pluralistic as the Western capitalist orientation is individualistic. In other words, not only does the individualistic heritage of the West fail to account for the full range of human experience, an entire world view may be successfully built on its very opposite.[15]

The real question to be faced by those of us in the Western tradition and by others who may be affected or influenced by our world view is whether or not, to put it in Hsu's terms, the affective dimension of the Western tradition, long neglected and, one suspects, badly atrophied from disuse, can be revitalized in some fashion. Some observers would make "a return to traditional values" a necessary precondition to curing the modern malaise.[16] However, such prescriptions—which so often take the form of proscriptions on certain forms of behavior that are thought to violate "traditional values"—generally reflect an extremely shallow view of what tradition consists of. Despite memory's attempt to convince us that the past was a better time, there is simply no tradition of affect to which the Western capitalist tradition can "return," were such a return even possible. At least since the Reformation, and probably long before that, our traditions in the West have been decidedly and triumphantly individualistic; the disappearance of the gemeinschaft of which Tonnies speaks was a consequence not of abandonment of traditional values but of the pursuit of a logical line of thought, itself part of a centuries-old tradition that we have inherited. That tradition, as we have seen, progressed in no small part at the expense of the social and interactive side of humankind, thus narrowing considerably the possibility that affect can emerge, let alone be "returned to." There is, quite simply, no going back.

But need we despair about going forward? Here again, it is important to keep in mind that a prognosis is all we can hope to develop— and a highly tentative one at that. We should begin by amending somewhat Ruth Benedict's objection to the belief that what is subtracted from society is added to the individual (see chapter 8). It is clear that, though we can keep no neat accounting that weighs the demands of society against the needs of the individual, an extreme emphasis on one will necessarily take place at the expense of the other. Benedict is closer to the mark when she says that, in a meager society, the individual suffers, in a rich one he or she thrives. What is needed is a balance between the two, an equilibrium in which each reciprocally enriches the other. Moreover, we must also acknowledge the great fund of personal self-confidence available to the individual in the Western tradition, self-confidence that itself might be a great asset in attempting to introduce a more pluralistic world view as a step forward.[17] With those qualifications in mind, it might be valuable to look at one point of intersection between the individualistic and the pluralistic world views, one that suggests some interesting, even encouraging, developments.

Rogelio Diaz-Guerrero, a Mexican psychologist, has studied the psychology of children living along the U.S.-Mexican border—one of those rare places where a Western capitalistic culture and a more traditional, pluralistic culture meet, both in their natural habitat.[18] Using what he calls a "Views of Life" questionnaire designed to measure such things as obedience versus self-assertion, response to authority, and attitudes toward family, Diaz-Guerrero produced a profile of the children that was congruent with what one would expect from the work of both Dealy and Hsu: American children were found to be more active in dealing with life's problems, Mexican children were more passive; Mexican children were more family centered, Americans were more self-centered; Americans were more competitive, Mexicans were more cooperative. But much more dramatic was the finding that the closer a subject lived to the border, and thus to the culture that existed on the other side, the more his or her cultural characteristics were tempered with elements of the other side. In other words, diffusion of the cultural values of each side was taking place across the border.

Perhaps even more encouragingly, at least where the problem of the circularity of modern individualism is concerned, diffusion of Mexican values among Anglo children seemed stronger than diffusion in the opposite direction.[19] The dominant direction of this diffusion is not hard to understand. Diaz-Guerrero remarks that "there is a great fear of loss of identity in both Americans and Mexicans if they dare to imitate or assimilate characteristics of the other group." However, if, as we suggested above, the triumph of individualism has produced a self eminently capable of its own powers, one would expect American children to be less threatened by an encounter with something that is out of the range of their own cultural experience and less threatened by loss of identity as they assimilate it. Diaz-Guerrero remarks that the process of assimilation may be fine if the positive aspects of each culture are what is assimilated by its counterpart, but there is no guarantee that will be the case; nonetheless, he concludes that "selective assimilation of the positive aspects of the other culture can only produce better Mexicans, better Americans."[20]

Such findings are not unique.[21] Moreover, they may represent some cause for optimism among those to whom the decline of individualism may have seemed to signal imminent decline in the West. However, we must be very cautious about how we treat them. To begin with, there is nothing to suggest that extrapolation from studies such as those done by Diaz-Guerrero to inferences about the shift from individualism to pluralism in the Western world are justified. To make such inferences runs the risk of introducing a deus ex machina that appears to resolve a variety of problems, while it may in fact resolve none. The extent to which a pluralistic vision can, when those who hold it are pushed to extreme positions, lead to fanaticism has also been demonstrated by cults and despots with alarming frequency in our own time; and so has the extent to which an individualistic frame of mind can still, in certain circumstances, remain a beacon on a frighteningly dark horizon.[22] Only history—and probably history over great stretches of time—can answer the question of whether or not the encounter between the individualistic, capitalistic West and cultures from more pluralistic traditions is likely to provide new impetus to both.

But like any good physician, having made a prognosis in a difficult case, we are free to—perhaps even bound to—find support for it. In this case, there certainly seems to be support. If the birth of consciousness was, as we have said, the event that sowed the seeds of individualism, and if that event took place, as Jaynes maintains, as a product of the encounter between cultures, then it would seem fair to consider that paradigm as a possible one as we search for the vehicle by which we might expect a shift out of the individualistic mode into a pluralistic one. In fact, essential to Jaynes's argument is the *contrast* that existed between the bicameral cultures that encountered one another and the way in which that contrast forced them into self-conscious awareness; similarly, it seems reasonable to argue that the encounter with cultures that hold pluralistic values above individualistic ones may make the individualistic among us more aware both of individualism's limitations and of the advantages of pluralism for the situation in which we currently find ourselves.[23]

Quite clearly, the Western capitalistic world view is desperately in need of something that will relieve the alienation, both from self and from society, that has increasingly plagued it for the last two centuries, and the heart of that alienation, as we have seen, seems to lie in the individualistic world view in which we have become trapped. Certainly the encounter with other cultures, which has become almost an inevitability in the contemporary global structure that has itself evolved as a product of the individualistic world view, affords one opportunity, not only for distracting us from our increasingly circular preoccupation with ourselves, but also for providing us the seeds of the pluralism that we must eventually begin to move toward.

Victor Frankl has remarked that the "crisis of meaning" in the West seems paradoxical in view of the fact that there are so many profoundly meaningful issues facing the human species when it is viewed in a global context. The great irony, he says, is that while today's Western youth express a desire to become involved with the problems of others but lack the vehicles for doing so, the vast majority of the earth's population remains in such dire need for the basics of life. Perhaps, Frankl speculates, "to the extent to which the First World sees its task in fighting the hunger in the Third World, it helps itself to overcome its own meaning crisis: We give them bread, they give us meaning—not a bad bargain."[24] In one respect, Frankl's remarks might be taken to be unintentionally patronizing: they smack, just slightly, of condescension on the part of the West toward what the Third World has to offer. But if we broaden the perspective of Frankl's remarks somewhat, they take on an intriguingly true ring.

If we see the world, not so much in terms of numbered domains of politics and economics, but in terms of the cultures of individualistic Western capitalism and its pluralistic counterparts, a curious complementarity seems to emerge. The characterization of the contemporary globe in terms of such a duality is implicit in L. S. Stavrianos's *Global Rift,* a work that demonstrates that the contemporary world political and economic structure is largely the product of the success of the forces mobilized in Europe by the Protestant/capitalist revolution, and that this structure has been "globalized"—it forces virtually all cultures into a position of interdependence and mutual encounter. Stavrianos's work is largely political and historical, but if we see it in cultural terms, it is not hard to imagine the evolution of individualism as a development that, in Hegelian-Marxian fashion, has so thoroughly succeeded in making itself felt that it has produced the means by which its own contradictions can be resolved.[25]

The emergence of global interdependency in economics and politics is largely a product, as Stavrianos demonstrates, of the network fashioned by the individualistic capitalism of Western Europe and, later, the United States. That same capitalism has also helped to contribute to the precipitous decline in the "affective" dimension Hsu attributes to societies with a more pluralistic world view. Yet at the same time, the network created by Western capitalism has created economic and political conditions that virtually guarantee, not only interaction with cultures that have more pluralistic world views than its own, but an increasing degree of such interaction over the long term.

The temptation to see inevitability in such developments is great but is generally one that must be resisted if one is to avoid either simplistic advocacy or a fatalistic passivity. This much, however, can be said: the individualistic worldview, which has brought the West to what Frankl calls a "meaning crisis," has also made virtually inevitable the encounter with cultures that offer an alternative to individualism. Moreover, individualism itself may have provided sufficient ego strength to allow those who live in its domain to selectively assimilate aspects of the pluralistic cultures they now encounter. But just as possibly, individualism may so fully limit their perception of the world that they fail to take the necessary steps to break out of the circularity it represents. In such a case, it would not be hard to imagine a world some time in the future dominated by those with the pluralistic world view that, for other reasons such as ecology, sharing of global resources, and the threat of annihilation through high-tech warfare, provides a perspective more appropriate to the contemporary problems faced by the human species.

Notes

Introduction

1. See Thomas Kuhn's *Structure of Scientific Revolutions* (Chicago: University of Chicago Press, 1962), especially chaps. 1 and 2.

2. There are many ways in which this topic can be sliced. David Lodge, in his *Working with Structuralism* (London: Routledge & Kegan Paul, 1981), distinguishes between "classical" and "post-classical" structuralists. Vytautas Kavolis, in a distinction related to that made here between traditional and transformational modes, suggests still another angle; see his "History of Consciousness and Civilization Analysis," *Comparative Civilizations Review,* no. 17 (Fall 1987): 1–19.

3. The term "individual subject," like others used by those who advocate a transformational approach to individualism, can lead to confusion—sometimes deliberate, as when Foucault employs it to denote the fiction of the self and to connote the subordination of that self to power relationships, aiming ultimately to dissolve the term's meaning altogether. This study aims at a conception more in line with that of Oliver Sacks, who complains that modern psychology often launders itself of the individuality of a subject/patient: "There is no 'subject' in a narrow case history," Sacks says; "modern case histories allude to the subject in a cursory phrase ('a trisonic albino female of 21') which could as well apply to a rat as a human being" (*The Man Who Mistook His Wife for a Hat* [New York: Harper & Row, 1987], p. 4).

4. An uneven but relatively readable introduction to some of the major elements treated superficially here is *An Introductory Guide to Post-Structuralism and Post-Modernism,* by Madan Sarup (Athens: University of Georgia Press, 1989). Probably the best and most comprehensive treatment of the work of Michel Foucault is *Michel Foucault: Beyond Structuralism and Hermeneutics,* by Hubert L. Dreyfus and Paul Rabinow, 2d ed. (Chicago: University of Chicago Press, 1983), a work that suffers somewhat from the fact that its authors, admirers of Foucault, sometimes get wrapped in the opacity for which Foucault himself is known.

5. It could be said that a figure such as Jacques Lacan does indeed try to posit a fulcrum firm enough to move a reliable interpretive lever; however, Lacan is so deliberately obscure that one is tempted to agree with Charles Hampden-Turner when he says that most of Lacan's public statements "seem designed less to inform people than to beguile them into lengthy personal exploration under Lacanian auspices" (*Maps of the Mind* [New York: Macmillan, 1981], p. 156).

6. Walter Ong, *Orality and Literacy* (New York: Methuen, 1982), p. 167.

7. One could go further than Ong and argue that in such areas as literary criticism, structuralism has created a closed system based on terminological rigidity that suggests, not the limitations of language, but the limitations of language as it is used within the structuralist worldview. See, for example, Alison Lurie's lucid critique, "A Dictionary for Deconstructors," in *The State of the Language,* 2d ed., ed. L. Michaels and C. Ricks (Berkeley: University of California Press, 1990).

8. Though Derek Bickerton's *Language and Species* (Chicago: University of Chicago Press, 1990) takes a convincing step in the right direction, I have yet to see a discussion that responds to the poststructuralist/postmodernist critique with the reminder that, though language is not a clear window through which we perceive reality, it is, in the truest Darwinian sense, a product of a highly selective natural world: to assume that because it is a construct of human consciousness it is therefore permanently trapped in some hyperspace unrelated to the rest of the material cosmos is to slip into a kind of reverse Manichaean view that is tendentious at best. Kant's assertion of the categorical imperative (see below, chap. 6) may seem no better, but recent work such as that by neuropsychologist Karl Pribram and physicist David Bohm on the holographic structure that may underlie mind *and* matter suggests Kant may not have been far off the mark. See the special edition of *Revision* 1, no. 1 (1978) devoted to the work of Pribram and Bohm, as well as Pribram's *Languages of the Brain* (Monterey, Calif.: Brooks-Cole, 1977) and Bohm's "Quantum Theory as an Indication of a New Order in Physics: Implicate and Explicate Order in Physical Law," *Foundations of Physics,* no. 3 (1973): 139–168.

9. Ong, *Orality and Literacy,* p. 170.

10. Here again, Sacks's characterization of the clinical "subject" is apropos: "To restore the human subject at the centre—the suffering, afflicted, fighting, human subject—we must deepen a case history to a narrative or a tale; only then do we have a 'who' as well as a 'what', a real person, a patient, in relation to disease" (*Man Who Mistook His Wife,* p. viii).

11. An excellent discussion of the importance of this feature of written language is J. Goody and I. Watt's "Consequences of Literacy," in Goody's *Literacy in Traditional Societies* (Cambridge: Cambridge University Press, 1968).

12. In Jameson's view, the "individual consciousness" is actually a product of what Marx would call alienation—the fragmentation of human communality that takes place as a result of exploitative material relations. See Jameson's *Political Unconscious: Narrative as a Socially Symbolic Act* (Ithaca: Cornell University Press, 1981).

13. This question underlies recent controversy over "Western Civilization" courses in American universities. For an interesting discussion of the philosophical underpinnings to the controversy, see John Searle's "Battle over the University," *New York Review of Books* 37, no. 19 (December 6, 1990).

14. This is not to say that there may have lived countless Sapphos and Schopenhauers, Curies and Coplands in medieval hovels or Third World slums who, given the right circumstances, might have made brilliant contributions to the sum total of human knowledge and experience. It is only to underscore the role fate plays in giving talent a voice, as well as the importance of eliminating obstacles to the expression of talent wherever we can do so.

15. Modern investigative science has perhaps led us, falsely, to assume a high degree of intentionality in the development of technology. In fact, technology can be seen as an extension of what Weston La Barre has called "adaptive radiation", a basic feature of evolution, and one that involves intuition and dumb luck as often as it does intentionality; see his *Human Animal* (Chicago: University of Chicago Press, 1972). The fact that individualism was neither "invented," as was the incandescent bulb, nor applied by systematic design, as was the assembly line, does not diminish the fact that it emerged as a solution to a problem. On the question of the unwieldiness of large social entities, see Jane Jacobs's remarks on "economics of scale" in *The Question of Separatism* (New York: Random House, 1980).

16. A decade ago, as I was remarking on the limits of American individualism to a class of non-Americans, a student from a developing country reminded me that, while such concepts as individual prerogative may have become burdensome features of life in the West, they nonetheless provided a degree of self-confidence that allowed the individual to contribute to society as a whole—something he found sorely lacking in his own culture. His remark underlies much of what is said in this Introduction.

17. The strongly adversarial nature of some "unmasking" critiques often suggests that they are still heavily laden with the emotional import of disappointment that comes when the belief that is unmasked has been discovered to fall short of the believer's expectations. Carl Becker took note of the significance of belief in intellectual constructs half a century ago in *The Heavenly City of the Eighteenth Century Philosophers* (New Haven: Yale University Press, 1970), and his remarks still have much to tell us about the nature of belief in contemporary intellectual analysis.

18. Here again, the special use of the term "genealogy" by the likes of Foucault may make its use here confusing. However, there seems to be no better word for what is examined in this book: the "genesis" over time of the belief system known as individualism.

1. Toward a Redefinition of Individualism

1. Cited in Steven Lukes, *Individualism* (New York: Harper & Row, 1973), p. 29.

2. A. D. Lindsay, "Individualism," in *Encyclopaedia of the Social Sciences*

(New York: Macmillan, 1930–33), 7: 674. Though Lindsay does not necessarily mean "negative" in the pejorative sense, the difficulty in finding "positive" phrasing for those societies that foster individualism underscores the ambiguity of the term and the reasons for which it is often held in disfavor.

3. Colin Morris, *The Discovery of the Individual: 1050–1200* (New York: Harper & Row, 1972), p. 3.

4. Ibid.

5. Lukes, *Individualism*, pp. 43–44, vii–viii, 125.

6. Max Weber's remark about the value a "historically oriented conceptual analysis" of individualism is itself made as an aside to a discussion of religion— specifically, Puritan theology (see Max Weber, *The Protestant Ethic and the Spirit of Capitalism* [New York: Scribner's, 1958], p. 105 n. 22.), but Lukes includes only a brief discussion of what he calls "religious individualism," and his remarks offer nothing to suggest—as Morris and Dumont believe—that religion may have played a fundamental role in the evolution of individualism.

7. David Riesman, *Selected Essays from Individualism Reconsidered* (New York: Anchor, 1954), p. 27.

8. Louis Dumont, *Essays on Individualism: Modern Ideology in Anthropological Perspective* (Chicago: University of Chicago Press, 1986), pp. 23–59.

9. See Lukes, *Individualism*, pp. 99–109.

10. Ian Watt, *The Rise of the Novel: Studies in Defoe, Richardson, and Fielding* (Berkeley: University of California Press, 1957), pp. 13, 12, 13 (emphasis added).

11. Individualism, Watt says, "posits a whole society mainly governed by the idea of every individual's intrinsic independence both from other individuals and from that multifarious allegiance to past modes of thought and action denoted by the word 'tradition'—a force that is always social, not individual," (ibid., p. 60).

12. The use of third person personal pronouns in this sentence points up a difficulty in word choice a topic like this presents. While sensitivity to gender issues calls for such usages as "him or her" where "him" once sufficed, in many cases the role of the individual had much more immediate consequence for males than it did for females, at least until the nineteenth century. One could rightly argue that to use "him or her" referring to the emergence of the individual before the nineteenth century stretches the truth considerably. Nonetheless, even where shades of meaning may be lost, gender-inclusive language has been chosen throughout.

13. Cited in Watt, *Rise of the Novel*, p. 225.

14. See Julian Jaynes's remarks in chapter 3 below on the emergence of consciousness as a function of perceiving differences between oneself and others.

15. Lukes calls his analysis "a conceptual map" but admits that it is "radically incomplete" (*Individualism*, p. 158).

2. The Ancient World

1. See the *Encyclopaedia of the Social Sciences*, p. 675.

2. Dumont, *Essays on Individualism*, p. 28.

3. Eric Fromm, *You Shall Be as Gods* (New York: Fawcett, 1966), p. 37.

4. See Freud's *Future of an Illusion* (New York: Bantam, 1967) for a complete discussion of how religions represent idealized human self-projections.

5. See Paul Johnson's discussion of the Hebrew conception of God in his *History of Christianity* (New York: Penguin, 1976), p. 10.

6. Walter Ong, in *Orality and Literacy,* seems to want to deflate Jaynes's findings somewhat by suggesting that "bicamerality may mean simply orality" (p. 30). But he goes on to admit that "the question of bicamerality and literacy perhaps needs further investigation." Jaynes's book is, however, one of only two citations under the heading "consciousness" in *The Oxford Companion to the Mind;* many, like Neil Postman in *Amusing Ourselves to Death* (New York: Penguin, 1985), pp. 165–66 n. 7, and Charles Hampden-Turner in *Maps of the Mind,* pp. 90–93, take Jaynes at face value.

7. Julian Jaynes, *The Emergence of Consciousness in the Breakdown of the Bicameral Mind* (New York: Houghton-Mifflin, 1976), p. 55 (emphasis added).

8. Ibid., pp. 269, 263.

9. Ibid., p. 73. Jaynes means by "lexical field" a group of words that, by virtue of their ready availability to a speaker or writer for signification, description, etc., indicate the familiarity of the experience or thing that they are commonly used to identify. Psychoanalysis, for example, uses such terms as "ego," "id," and "superego" to indicate aspects of the human personality; their use emerges from the psychoanalytic conviction that personality reveals certain characterics that these terms designate. More technical and avowedly precise than that which Jaynes says emerged among the Greeks, psychoanalytic terminology nonetheless represents a lexical field that, by virtue of its widespread acceptance in whole or in part, establishes more elusive aspects of personality as though they were tangible objects. Frederic Jameson's discussion of psychoanalytic terminology in *Political Unconscious,* pp. 58–74, explores some of the hermeneutical difficulties created when two lexical fields (in this case, those of psychoanalysis and Marxism) collide and create "cross-talk."

10. Jaynes, *Emergence of Consciousness,* p. 274.

11. Ibid., pp. 276, 219.

12. Ibid., pp. 281, 280, 283.

13. Ibid., pp. 286, 287.

14. Ibid., p. 260. Briefly, Jaynes's categories describe the words used by the Greeks, for instance, as more or less metaphoric. Those that are least metaphoric he calls objective, because they refer to actual "things," like breathing; those that are most metaphoric he calls subjective, because they refer to mental processes. Jaynes is thus characterizing the words themselves with his nomenclature. I propose to characterize the state of mind of the speaker/writer of the words, thus making the emergence of consciousness the first "subjective" moment in our psychic history. This usage reverses the polarity of Jaynes's nomenclature without changing its substance.

15. This concept of a "buffer" between the individual and experience parallels Freud's description of the development of the ego in *Beyond the Pleasure Principle* (New York: Bantam, 1967).

16. Jaynes, *Emergence of Consciousness,* pp. 293–313.

17. Ibid., pp. 239–41.

18. Ibid., p. 296.

19. Ibid., pp. 141–75.

20. Ibid., p. 299.

21. Karl Pribram has suggested to me that a paramount gap in Jaynes's account is his failure to recognize the significance of the development of the alphabet in the emergence of any analog form of self-concept. This same criticism is implied in Walter Ong's statement (see n. 6 above).

22. Jaynes, *Emergence of Consciousness,* pp. 141–75.

23. Fromm's analysis places heavy emphasis on the extent to which Hebraism established a free individual.

24. Jaynes, *Emergence of Consciousness,* pp. 217, 211. Jaynes notes that this view conflicts with the tradition in philosophy of inferring the consciousness of others from the awareness of one's own, but we need not solve this riddle to recognize the correspondence between Morris's remark and Jaynes's. Moreover, as Jaynes himself notes, his view parallels in many respects the view of those, such as George Herbert Mead, who see self-consciousness as a product of social, rather than strictly personal, forces; see chapter 8 below.

3. Christianity

1. Morris, *Discovery of the Individual,* p. 13. W. H. McNeill remarks on a "mass of culturally dispossessed individuals, who found themselves psychologically alienated from established religious and cultural values," among which "the great and truly world-shaking traditions found fertile ground" (*The Rise of the West* [New York: Mentor, 1963], pp. 364–65). Paul Johnson describes the same shift in a more positive light (*History of Christianity,* p. 7).

2. Dumont, *Essays on Individualism,* p. 28. Unfortunately, Dumont jumps immediately to another unhelpful conclusion; see above, chapter 1.

3. Jaynes, *Emergence of Consciousness,* p. 176. See also Ong, *Orality and Literacy.*

4. Jaynes, *Emergence of Consciousness,* pp. 208, 302.

5. Paul Johnson remarks that "in a sense . . . the law was God" (*History of Christianity,* p. 14); see also the discussion entitled "From History to the Law" in Thomas Sheehan's *First Coming: How the Kingdom of God Became Christianity* (New York: Dorset, 1986) pp. 35–38, and Fromm, *You Shall Be as Gods,* pp. 41–46.

6. Jaynes, *Emergence of Consciousness,* p. 318.

7. See, for example, discussions in Morris, *Discovery of the Individual;* Dumont, *Essays on Individualism;* and the *Encyclopaedia of the Social Sciences;* see also John E. Smith, "The Individual and the Judeo-Christian Tradition," in *The Status of the Individual in East and West,* ed. Charles A. Moore (Honolulu: University of Hawaii Press, 1968).

8. This view is more clearly apparent in modern translations, where, for instance, Matthew 6:18 is rendered, "your Father who is in the secret place,"

rather than "your Father who is in secret" (*The New English Bible* [New York: Cambridge University Press, 1961]), emphasizing a kind of mind-space—rather than the temple—as a place of worship. See also Elaine Pagels's discussion "Gnosis: Self-Knowledge as Knowledge of God," in *The Gnostic Gospels* (New York: Vintage, 1981).

9. Many such features of Christianity take on their more fully spatialized and temporalized forms over time, as codification and elaboration of the early Christian message takes place (see chap. 4 below).

10. See n. 8.

11. McNeill says, "A pervasive historicity of outlook also distinguished Christianity. . . . Christians regarded the Creation, Incarnation and Last Judgement as unique events which gave meaning and hope to ordinary terrestrial human life" (*Rise of the West*, p. 368). Sheehan, speaking from a highly modern perspective, faults Christianity for historicizing what he feels was Jesus' real, more timeless message (see *First Coming*, pp. 221–27); in any case, the cosmic chronology introduced by Christianity is a clear example of what Jaynes calls narratization (see *Emergence of Consciousness*, p. 65).

12. Jaynes, *Emergence of Consciousness*, p. 346.

13. While I am not familiar with the Old Testament scholarship on this question, it would seem, for instance, that the nature of goodness in the Old Testament is of a more static quality than in the New Testament. Not that the Old Testament ignores magnitudes of goodness; but the New Testament is vastly more oriented toward the complexities of human behavior than the Old and thus allows for the possibility (indeed, almost necessitates) a "sliding scale" upon which quality of character can be measured.

14. This tradition, however, is not necessarily sustained in later church theology. See Pagels, "Gnosis."

15. See Jaynes, *Emergence of Consciousness*, chap. 1, book 3: "The Quest for Authorization."

16. John Freccero, "Autobiography and Narrative," in *Reconstructing Individualism,* ed. Thomas C. Heller et al. (Stanford: Stanford University Press, 1986), pp. 16–17.

17. Johnson, *History of Christianity*, p. 122. Elaine Pagels develops this point exhaustively in her *Adam, Eve, and the Serpent* (New York: Random House, 1988).

18. Freccero, "Autobiography and Narrative," p. 21. See also Jaynes's remarks about Augustine (*Emergence of Consciousness*, p. 2).

19. Note also the figurative, parable-filled discourse with which Jesus delivered his message.

20. Freccero, "Autobiography and Narrative," pp. 22 (emphasis added), 17.

21. Morris, *Discovery of the Individual*, p. 11.

22. Ibid., p. 12.

23. See Sigmund Freud, *Moses and Monotheism* (New York: Vintage, 1939), p. 134; see also Fromm's remark that "the Talmudic sages and their successors . . . did not expect, or even want, the other nations of the world to adopt the Jewish faith" (*You Shall Be as Gods*, p. 41).

24. See Freud, *Group Psychology and the Analysis of the Ego* (New York: Norton, 1959).

25. This feature of Christ's message survived in no small part thanks to Paul's insistence that Mosaic law need not apply in the early church, thus opening up the conversion of the Gentiles; see Johnson, *History of Christianity,* pp. 35–43; McNeill, *Rise of the West,* p. 370. Elaine Pagels also illustrates the extent to which orthodox Christianity's opposition to gnostic "heresies" eliminated spiritual differentiation within the church, a differentiation that, while increasing the individualistic potential for a chosen few, would have relegated the mass of believers to second-class status and thus made Paul's attempts at proselytizing much more difficult. In fact, Pagels demonstrates how the defeat of the potentially anarchic approach to Christian truth posited by the gnostics allowed a wider dispersal of the individualistic core of that truth, albeit at the expense of its subtler features; see *The Gnostic Gospels,* especially pp. 138–42.

26. See Neill, *The History of Christian Missions* (London: Pelican, 1986).

4. The Middle Ages and the Renaissance

1. See Johnson, *History of Christianity;* Dieter Georgi, *Opponents of Paul in II Corinthians* (London: T. & T. Clark, 1986).

2. An interesting elaboration of this now rather commonplace view is Thomas Sheehan's *First Coming.*

3. Morris, *Discovery of the Individual,* pp. 64, 66.

4. Ibid., p. 67.

5. Ibid., p. 68.

6. Ibid., pp. 69, 70.

7. Ibid., p. 73.

8. Ibid., pp. 74–75, 76. See also Eric Fromm's comments on "the legitimacy of the expression of [the individual's] whole self" in the Middle Ages in his *Escape from Freedom* (New York: Avon, 1969), p. 91.

9. Morris, *Discovery of the Individual,* pp. 76–79.

10. Jacob Burckhardt, *The Civilization of the Renaissance in Italy* (New York: New American Library, 1960), p. 121. See Walter Ullman, *The Individual and Society in the Middle Ages* (Baltimore: Johns Hopkins University Press, 1966).

11. See Natalie Zemon Davis's comments on Burckhardt in her essay "Boundaries and the Sense of Self in Sixteenth Century France," in *Reconstructing Individualism,* ed. Heller et al.

12. Burckhardt, *Civilization,* pp. 226–28.

13. Ibid., p. 250.

14. Morris, *Discovery of the Individual,* pp. 87, 95.

15. Burckhardt, *Civilization,* p. 249.

16. This tendency can be traced back to a reviving of Vetruvius's ancient belief that, as Kenneth Clark puts it, "man's body is a model of proportion" (*The Nude* [London: John Murray, 1973], p. 13).

17. Burckhardt, *Civilization,* p. 241.

18. Morris, *Discovery of the Individual*, p. 85.

19. Burckhardt, *Civilization*, pp. 128, 129, 364.

20. Ibid., pp. 356–86, 320.

21. Morris, *Discovery of the Individual*, pp. 64, 65.

22. Burckhardt, *Civilization*, p. 241.

23. In essence, the human tendency toward objectification began with the world beyond the self: "objects" that once may have terrified humankind, attracted it, or simply been ignored by it became subject to careful scrutiny—increasingly systematic scrutiny once the scientific method developed—as increasing self-confidence encouraged the individual to trust his or her powers of observation and analysis. Inevitably, the self itself became an object of systematic scrutiny. However, as we shall see below (chaps. 7 and 8), scrutiny of the self has the curious effect of enlarging the domain of the self, producing new passages in the labyrinth even as it explores; thus "absolute" objectivity about the self became a kind of mathematical impossibility.

24. We might, in fact, go so far as to offer the immersion-subjectivity-objectivity axis as a paradigm for much of what we have seen thus far in the genealogy of individualism: physical experience, in which the individual was once immersed, gives way to subjective consciousness—the awareness of experience; eventually, that awareness itself gives way to objectivity—a kind of deliberate, or deliberated, awareness of experience—almost as though it had itself become the mode in which the individual was now immersed.

5. The Reformation

1. Fromm, *Escape from Freedom*, pp. 120–21, 60, 81.

2. Ibid., p. 121.

3. Weber, *Protestant Ethic*, pp. 24, 17.

4. Ibid., pp. 51, 79–92, 95–183.

5. Ibid., pp. 17, 102–3.

6. Ibid., pp. 103–4.

7. Ibid., pp. 111, 113 (emphasis added), 115.

8. Ibid., pp. 158, 159, 172, 176. Weber argues that, while other forms of Protestantism such as Pietism, Methodism, and the Baptist sects do not necessarily reveal the traits antecedent to Western capitalism that he finds in Calvin and the Puritans, his emphasis on the latter is justified by the fact that they played the most influential role in making Western capitalistic attitudes palatable to Europeans and later to North Americans. See his chapter 4, "The Religious Foundations of Worldly Asceticism," pp. 95–154.

9. Ibid., pp. 111 (emphasis added), 121, 110.

10. Ibid., p. 114.

11. Ibid., pp. 176, 109.

12. Ibid., pp. 157–58.

13. See Jaynes, *Emergence of Consciousness*, pp. 250–51.

14. Macfarlane raises this issue with a somewhat different point in mind. He tries to demonstrate that England's experience was different from that of

continental Europe, that individual ownership and primogeniture existed in England before the influences to which they have been attributed in Western Europe. His analysis is convincing, but he disappointingly fails to account for the difference. In any event, his discussion merely adds detail to the larger picture, showing us ways in which England's difference ultimately accelerated the process we are here describing. However, his analysis does not—as he seems to think (see his *Origins of English Individualism* [Oxford: Blackwell, 1978], pp. 198–99)—successfully demonstrate that individualism was antecedent to capitalism, at least as Weber defines it (see Weber, *Protestant Ethic,* pp. 19–31).

15. Macfarlane, *Origins,* p. 23. He is actually quoting W. I. Thomas and F. Znaniecki, *The Polish Peasant* (New York: Dover, 1958).

16. Weber, *Protestant Ethic,* pp. 117, 17, 25, 27.

17. Ibid., p. 124.

18. Fromm, *Escape from Freedom,* p. 111.

19. See Jaynes, *Emergence of Consciousness,* pp. 236–46.

20. Weber, *Protestant Ethic,* p. 107.

21. Fromm, *Escape from Freedom,* p. 119.

22. Weber, *Protestant Ethic,* p. 108.

23. Fromm, *Escape from Freedom,* p. 115.

6. The Age of Individualism

1. Suzanne Langer, *Philosophy in a New Key* (New York: Mentor, 1948), p. 177.

2. The organization of Lukes's book is somewhat confusing in this respect, for under the heading "The Basic Ideas of Individualism," he includes both ideas that underlie individualistic attitudes (Autonomy, Privacy, The Dignity of Man) and specific *kinds* of individualism (Political Individualism, Economic Individualism, etc.).

3. See works cited earlier and in this chapter by Dumont, Lukes, Macpherson, Macfarlane, and Watt. Lukes, however, does not use the term "possessive," and Watt's discussion subsumes political ideas within a literary analysis.

4. Weber, *Protestant Ethic,* p. 111 (emphasis added).

5. See Richard Tawney's *Religion and the Rise of Capitalism* (New York: Harcourt Brace, 1926), pp. 227–53, for a detailed analysis of how Puritanism developed the economic aspects of Calvinism into a program for productive economic activity.

6. C. B. Macpherson, *The Political Theory of Possessive Individualism: Hobbes to Locke* (Oxford: Oxford University Press, 1964), pp. 263, 264.

7. Admittedly, the seventeenth century spoke, at least nominally, with the understanding that God remained somewhere in the background of human reality. But as Weber and others suggest, the significance of God's place in human affairs is marginal and becomes increasingly so as the trends that appear in the seventeenth century eventually lead to a complete secularization of philosophy and epistemology as early as Hume, a century later.

8. Macpherson, *Political Theory* p. 264 (emphasis added); see his chapters 3–5.

9. Dumont's discussion is, in this regard, only slightly more comprehensive than Lukes's.

10. Macpherson concludes his book (pp. 271–77) with a succinct discussion of the contradictions that underlie liberal-democratic theories that base themselves on the assumptions of possessive individualism.

11. See Burckhardt, *Civilization,* pp. 211–17.

12. Johnson, *History of Christianity,* p. 319.

13. Watt, *Rise of the Novel,* p. 12.

14. E. W. F. Tomlin, *The Western Philosophers: An Introduction* (London: Hutchinson, 1968), p. 203.

15. Lukes, *Individualism,* pp. 107–9.

16. Morse Peckham, *Beyond the Tragic Vision: The Quest for Identity in the Nineteenth Century* (New York: Braziller, 1962), p. 96.

17. The distinction made here is intended to parallel exactly that made in grammar and lexicology. Lexical meaning focuses on roots: *plays, played, playing.* Grammatical meaning focuses on variations of the root: play*s,* play*ed,* play*ing.* In lexis, meaning emerges from a static quality; in grammar, it hinges on qualitative transformations that themselves depend on relationships, though grammar itself does not allow predication (affirmation, denial, etc.); only syntax makes that possible. (For a lucid explanation of how lexis becomes grammatical, see Bickerton, *Language and Species,* pp. 25–74). Thus, the ancient analog-I represents a simple denotation, but the Christian authorized self represents an entity that may be qualitatively transformed into various states.

18. Though not itself without problematic ambiguities. See Jaynes, *Emergence of Consciousness,* pp. 288–92, where Jaynes discusses the shift in the meaning of "*psyche*" from "life" to "soul."

19. These include everything from the distinction between "mortal" and "venial" sin to distinctions between heaven, hell, and "purgatory," and the various "indulgences" that afford one a state of increased spiritual well-being.

20. Technically, syntax falls within the larger category of grammar, while lexicology does not. My usage represents a slight variation from standard linguistic terminology; however, there is no other word that so appropriately expresses the step-increase in complexity represented by the innovations of Kant and those who followed him.

21. Here, too, Kant departs from the simple mechanism of the Enlightenment, which can be said to have inherited and accepted too much of Christianity's mechanical "grammar" in both its positive and negative forms.

22. W. L. Reese, *Dictionary of Philosophy and Religion* (Atlantic Highlands, N.J.: Humanities Press, 1980), p. 277.

23. Even in such terms as Freudian "cathexis" (a mistranslation that should actually be rendered "graded potential"), one can see a strong resemblance to Kant's own gradient scale.

24. See Lilian R. Furst, *Romanticism* (London: Methuen, 1976), pp. 1–14.

25. Crane Brinton, "Romanticism," in *The Encyclopedia of Philosophy* (New York: Macmillan, 1972), 7:206.

26. Lilian Furst, *Romanticism in Perspective* (London: Macmillan, 1969), p. 58, quoted in Lukes, *Individualism*, p. 68.

27. Quoted in Lukes, *Individualism*, p. 68.

28. As Brinton puts it, "The Romantic youth absorbed in the depths of Wordsworth's *Prelude*, or Chateaubriand's *Genie du Christianisme*, or Goethe's *Faust* felt nothing but contempt for the abstract ideas and the confined tastes of his shallow Voltairean grandfather" ("Romanticism," p. 207).

29. Lukes, *Individualism*, p. 67.

30. William Wordsworth, *The Prelude* (Rinehart Edition, edited by Carlos Baker, 1954), book 14, lines 89–95, 113–16.

31. M. H. Abrams, *Natural Supernaturalism* (New York: Norton, 1971), p. 96.

32. Quoted in Abrams *Mirror and the Lamp* (New York: Norton, 1953), p. 54.

33. Ibid., p. 50.

34. Wordsworth, *Prelude*, book 13, lines 287–93; book 1, lines 53–54.

35. Frank Kermode, *The Romantic Image* (London: Routledge & Kegan Paul, 1966), pp. 6, 7 (quoting Hazlitt).

36. Abrams, *Natural Supernaturalism*, p. 145.

7. From Individualism to Authenticity

1. See Peckham, *Beyond the Tragic Vision*.

2. See Wylie Sypher, *Loss of the Self in Modern Literature and Art* (New York: Vintage, 1962), p. 26.

3. Lionel Trilling, *Sincerity and Authenticity* (Cambridge: Harvard University Press, 1972), p. 2.

4. Ibid., p. 16.

5. Ibid., p. 26.

6. Ibid., p. 60.

7. Ibid., pp. 93–94.

8. Earlier, Trilling suggests that "society" is a phenomenon of relatively recent origin, "different from a kingdom or realm; and even a 'commonwealth,' as Hobbes uses that term." Society, says Trilling, is accessible to the critical understanding of individuals and susceptible to change (ibid., pp. 19, 26).

9. *Webster's New Collegiate Dictionary* (Springfield, Mass.: G. & C. Merriam, 1959), p. 59.

10. Trilling, *Sincerity and Authenticity*, p. 1.

11. Quoted in Macpherson, *Political Theory*, p. 76.

12. Trilling, *Sincerity and Authenticity*, pp. 109–10.

13. See ibid., pp. 102–5.

14. For a comprehensive view of Trilling and his critics and supporters, see Thomas Bender's "Trilling and American Culture," *American Quarterly* 42, no. 2 (June 1990): 324–47.

15. Trilling, *Sincerity and Authenticity,* p. 99.

16. See above, chapter 1.

17. See Trilling, pp. 19–25. Trilling seems to have erroneously taken Lacan to have attributed what he calls "the mirror stage" to the *manufacture* of mirrors in history; see Lacan's "Mirror Stage as Formative of the Function of the I," in *Ecrits: A Selection,* trans. Alan Sheridan (New York: Norton, 1977). See also Trilling's chapter 6, "The Authentic Unconscious."

18. Albert Camus, *The Myth of Sisyphus* (New York: Random House, 1955), p. 11.

19. Perhaps the classic statement of how this replication reflects the meaninglessness of so-called postmodern life is Frederic Jameson's "Postmodernism; or, The Cultural Logic of Late Capitalism," *The New Left Review,* no. 146 (July/ August 1984).

20. See chapter 2 above.

21. Sartre's notion of the individual's inescapable subjectivity is a typical example of this attitude.

22. See Philip Rieff, *Freud: The Mind of the Moralist* (Garden City, N.Y.: Anchor, 1961).

23. See Daniel Yankelovitch and William Barrett, *Ego and Instinct* (New York: Random House, 1970).

24. See my "Freud and Individualism," *Partisan Review* 59, no. 1 (Winter 1992). The emotional loading that exists on the topic of a thinker's "individualistic" or "anti-individualistic" tendencies is perhaps underscored by the curious history of this essay. Originally "enthusiastically" accepted by *Psychoanalytic Review,* the journal that first published Freud's own papers in English, a subsequent (and apparently heated) discussion of the paper brought about a reversal of the board's decision, even though the article had reached the stage of corrected proofs; the reason given was that Freud and psychoanalysis were committed to the nurturing of the self in all its fullness and could therefore not be "anti-individualistic."

25. Trilling, *Sincerity and Authenticity,* p. 157.

26. Ibid., p. 171.

8. Escaping the Labyrinth of the Self

1. Sartre's Introduction to his *Emotions: The Outline of a Theory* (New York: Philosophical Library, 1948), pp. 1–21, provides an excellent example of both the phenomenological and the existential approaches.

2. This discussion will, no doubt, disappoint some readers in its failure to treat at any length the work of Michel Foucault and those who, like him, argue that the very concepts of subject and self are the products of power relationships and therefore more to be dispelled through analysis than validated by "humanistic" interpretation. Much of what has been said here parallels closely such things as Foucault's discussion of the transition from "the classical self to the modern subject" (*The Foucault Reader* [New York: Pantheon, 1984],

pp. 350–72). In that respect, Foucault's work is certainly within the anti-individualistic tradition that has emerged in the last century and a half.

However, Foucault's importance is as much epistemological as analytical, and his epistemology, challenging as it does the validity of traditional psychology and anthropology—disciplines central to the epistemological bias represented in this discussion—probably makes our two approaches irreconcilable. The present discussion, like Jaynes's, assumes continuity of psychological features of human development over time. Approaches such as Foucault's demonstrate, as Walter Ong puts it, "little concern with historical continuities (which are psychological continuities)" (*Orality and Literacy,* p. 166). See also the remarks above in the Introduction.

3. See, for instance, R. D. Laing's *Divided Self* (Chicago: Quadrangle Books, 1960).

4. Rieff, *Freud,* p. 75.

5. John Dewey, *Individualism Old and New* (New York: Milton, Balch, 1930), pp. 90, 165, 166. In fairness to Dewey, it should be said that, as a pragmatist, he shares many of the assumptions about the relationship between the individual and society expressed by Mead (see the discussion of Mead below). Thus Dewey tries to focus, though with limited success, on what has been called the "individual-in-context" (H. S. Thayer, *Meaning and Action: A Critical History of Pragmatism* [New York: Bobbs-Merrill, 1968], p. 442).

6. *Marx's Concept of Man,* ed. Eric Fromm (New York: Frederick Ungar, 1966), p. 28. Fromm does, however, suggest that Marx represents the "full realization of individualism" (p. 3), but as Michael Harrington points out in chapter 6 of his *Twilight of Capitalism* (New York: Simon & Schuster, 1976), this is a result of Fromm's well-intentioned but overcompensatory attempt to reestablish Marx's spiritual side.

7. Lukes discusses some of the contrasts between Marxism and political individualism in his *Individualism,* pp. 85–87.

8. *Marx and Engels: Basic Writings on Politics and Philosophy,* ed. Lewis S. Feuer (New York: Anchor, 1959), p. 247.

9. M. H. Abrams perceptively notes what he calls a "consonance-in-difference" between Marx and the Romantics in their "humanistic naturalism" (*Natural Supernaturalism,* pp. 313–16).

10. *Marx's Concept of Man,* pp. 197, 203.

11. Jaynes, *Emergence of Consciousness,* p. 217. See above, chapter 1.

12. In this regard, however, Plato's remarks about love in *The Symposium* would seem to indicate that we retain some related residual memory.

13. Here too it must be said that such things as the Christian emphasis on the transformational quality of love suggests that the development we have traced was not an absolutely narcissistic one.

14. This scenario might help to explain the incredibly haunting power of works of fiction, such as the short stories of Nathaniel Hawthorne, in which a character like Young Goodman Brown or Reuben Bourne is exposed to an experience that undermines his ability to accept the "givens" of his society and permanently separates him from his fellows.

15. Ruth Benedict, *Patterns of Culture* (New York: Mentor, 1947), p. 232.
16. Ibid.
17. Chester Chard, *Man in Prehistory* (New York: McGraw-Hill, 1969), p. 67.
18. Jaynes mentions this similarity (*Emergence of Consciousness*, p. 74), though only in passing.
19. George Herbert Mead, *Mind, Self, and Society* (Chicago: University of Chicago Press, 1962), p. 175.
20. "I cannot turn around quick enough to catch myself," Mead says (ibid., p. 174).
21. Ibid., p. 35.
22. Chard, *Man in Prehistory*, p. 1 (emphasis added).

9. Beyond Individualism

1. I have in mind here such books as Marilyn Ferguson's *Aquarian Conspiracy* (London: Routledge & Kegan Paul, 1981), but also more serious works such as Charles Reich's *Greening of America* (Middlesex: Penguin, 1971) and L. S. Stavrianos's *Promise of the Coming Dark Age* (San Francisco: Freeman, 1976).
2. It is interesting to note that the *Encyclopedia of Philosophy* dates the first use of the word "socialism" as 1827, five years before the date generally recognized as the end of the Romantic period in literature.
3. This is not an argument, veiled or otherwise, for quietism. It is only to suggest that "praxis" requires that we first objectively assess the reality we intend to influence with our actions before we set out to do so.
4. Macfarlane, *Origins*, pp. 206, 170. (This quotation is a fusion of Macfarlane's own remark and his quotation of Montesquieu, which appear in separate parts of the text; the fusion, however, maintains the sense of both.)
5. See, for instance Edward Hall's *Silent Language* (New York: Anchor, 1972), Glen Fisher's *Mindsets: The Role of Culture and Perception in International Relations* (Yarmouth, Maine: Intercultural Press, 1988), and Geert Hofstede's *Culture's Consequences: International Differences in Work-Related Values* (Newbury Park, Calif.: Sage, 1984), to name but a few.
6. Glen Caudill Dealy, *The Public Man* (Amherst: University of Massachusetts Press, 1977), pp. 74, 82 (emphasis added).
7. Ibid., p. 81. Dealy's assessment is borne out by another writer, Octavio Paz, who, writing directly from the milieu of "the public man," develops a critique of the public orientation by arguing that the public self has grown hollow in contemporary Mexico, a "mask" behind which one hides one's deepest being, both from one's fellows and from oneself (*The Labyrinth of Solitude: Life and Thought in Mexico* [New York: Grove Press, 1960]).
8. Francis L. K. Hsu, *Rugged Individualism Reconsidered* (Knoxville: University of Tennessee Press, 1983), chapter 14, "The Effect of Dominant Kinship Relationships on Kin and Non-Kin Behavior: A Hypothesis," pp. 216–39; quotation on p. 263.

9. Ibid., p. 263.

10. Ibid., pp. 278, 280. Hsu is quoting himself here from an earlier work, *Clan, Caste, and Club* (Princeton: Van Nostrand-Reinhold, 1963).

11. See above, chapter 7.

12. Martin Yang, "The Concept of *Pao* as a Basis for Social Relations in China," in *Chinese Thought and Institutions,* ed. John K. Fairbank (Chicago: University of Chicago Press, 1957).

13. Hsu, *Rugged Individualism,* p. 289.

14. See Hofstede's analysis of individualistic and nonindividualistic work-related values (*Culture's Consequences,* chap. 5); see also Peter Adler's interesting essay "Beyond Cultural Identity: Reflections on Cultural and Multicultural Man," in *Topics in Culture Learning* 2 (August 1974).

15. I will not here engage the question of whether the Western individualistic tradition is "superior" to pluralistic traditions by virtue of its ability to introduce change; both Hsu and Dealy deal with that question extensively. Suffice it to say that individualism was certainly the tradition that allowed the West to achieve modernity, no small accomplishment. But whether or not it is the tradition to carry humankind further remains to be seen.

16. These calls are not restricted to political diatribe or religious revivalism. See, for instance, Robert Bellah et al., *Habits of the Heart: Individualism and Commitment in American Life* (New York: Harper & Row, 1985), as well as my discussion of the book in *Social Science Journal* 24, no. 3 (1987): 229–31.

17. Seen from this perspective, a truly humanistic Marxism might be just such a courageous step forward.

18. Rogelio Diaz-Guerrero, "Mexicans and Americans: Two Worlds, One Border . . . and One Observer," in *Views across the Border: The United States and Mexico,* ed. Stanley Ross (Albuquerque: University of New Mexico Press, 1978). This article includes findings published in previous papers.

19. In reference to a questionnaire on the meaning of the word "respect," the research found that "three items diffused from Mexico to the United States while only one diffused from the United States to Mexico" (ibid., p. 299).

20. Ibid., p. 302.

21. I have argued elsewhere that Diaz-Guerrero's findings may parallel what we know about the migrations of Indo-European tribes into the Roman Empire ("Migration in North America," paper presented to "Conference on the Americas," Louisiana Tech University, 1982), and that cultural diffusion of several kinds may be at work in the success Canada has enjoyed in dealing with Third World countries ("Canada, Quebec, and the Third World: Historical Liabilities and Improbable Success," *American Review of Canadian Studies* 17, no. 2 [1987]: 207–19). Stavrianos has made a much more sweeping assessment of the ascendancy of "third world values" in the global order in *Promise of the Coming Dark Age.*

22. See, for example, Vaclav Havel's *Letters to Olga* (London: Faber & Faber, 1988), only one of many instances in which a belief in the self genuinely sustains rather than traps one in an otherwise bleak modern landscape.

23. Because this is a discussion of a Western tradition of thought, we have

not addressed the ways in which pluralistic cultures may be affected by their encounter with the values of individualistic ones. Both Hsu and Diaz-Guerrero deal with this question. One need not think very hard to be reminded of the plethora of ways in which a pluralistic culture's encounter with the West may be to its disadvantage, not simply economically or politically, but in terms of the fragmentation of society and introduction of what are viewed as Western "vices"—some of which, we now know, come as much from modernization as from "cultural imperialism." However, one is led to speculate about whether or not cultures with a long tradition of pluralism may, in the very long run, be more fit to deal with the problems of modernization than those with an individualistic tradition—just as those with the ego-strength necessary for adoption of contrasting values may, as we saw, be in a better position to benefit from pluralism.

24. Victor Frankl, "The Meaning Crisis in the First World and Hunger in the Third World," *International Forum for Logotherapy* 7, no. 1 (Summer 1984): 7.

25. L. S. Stavrianos, *Global Rift* (New York: William Morrow, 1981). He later makes a case similar to the one we are suggesting here in his *Promise of the Coming Dark Age*.

Index